For

Hearts on Fire
*Fellowship of United Methodist Spiritual Directors
and Retreat Leaders*

CONTENTS

PREFACE

SPIRITUAL FORMATION HAPPENS all the time, whether we are aware of it or not. The culture in which we live; family, friends, and enemies; the technological, political, and social forces in the world, all these shape us as human beings, shape our spirit. At the same time, the triune God—God the Creator, the Son, and the Holy Spirit—surrounds us as individuals and as communities of faith. When we invite the Spirit into our lives, spiritual formation turns in a new direction. Christian spiritual formation is the process through which we become new creatures in Christ. Through the centuries Christians have sought and developed practices designed to be effective means for such formation.

During the past thirty years, various Christian denominations have embraced spiritual formation with renewed intensity as a distinct approach for cultivating Christian life. Resources and networks of persons have emerged. Spiritual Directors International has grown from a predominantly Roman Catholic organization to an ecumenical and interreligious network of more than sixty-five hundred members worldwide. Seminaries include courses in prayer practices, spiritual disciplines, and spiritual direction. The accrediting body for seminaries, the Association of Theological Schools, has listed "personal and spiritual formation" as a key criterion for seminary education since 1996. In practice, most Protestant seminaries have been serious about spiritual formation studies for only a little over a decade. Therefore, persons who have learned the rich legacy of prayer and spiritual disciplines may be laity attracted to this area of study, recent seminary graduates, and clergy who have pursued these studies in continuing education opportunities, such as Certification in Spiritual Formation, The Upper Room Academy for Spiritual Formation, or doctor of ministry programs.

In recent decades, the literature in spiritual formation has prolif-erated at an astonishing rate. I am particularly familiar with resources and programs offered by the United Methodist Church. The Upper Room, an ecumenical ministry of the United Methodist Board of Discipleship, has developed spiritual formation programs includ-ing the Walk to Emmaus, the Academy for Spiritual Formation, and Chrysalis, in addition to resources such as the Companions in Christ series. The UM Board of Discipleship also has supported the devel-opment of Covenant Discipleship Groups nationally. In 2000, the United Methodist Church approved the nationally recognized Certi-fication in Spiritual Formation. Many persons are now pursuing this specialized ministry as laypersons, in preparation for the ministry as deacons, or as continuing education for elders. Hearts on Fire: Fel-lowship of United Methodist Spiritual Directors and Retreat Leaders has been established as an affiliate organization of the United Meth-odist Church, under the sponsorship of Upper Room Ministries.

A Quiet Pentecost offers more than forty stories of inviting the Holy Spirit into congregational life. These voices come from United Methodist, Presbyterian, Episcopal, Missionary Baptist, Roman Cath-olic, African Methodist Episcopal, and United Church of Christ con-gregations, as well as retirement centers and campus ministries. All witness to the power of spiritual formation practices, whether in con-gregations, chaplaincy settings, or college campus ministries. These practices work! They are new wine, drawn from ancient sources. They enable people to experience a lived relationship with God and to grow in companionship and mission within their congregations and communities.

My gratitude is extended to each contributor for a pioneering spirit and generosity in sharing these stories. To the countless persons engaged in spiritual formation and spiritual direction ministries or curious about initiating them in their congregations, may this book be a source of affirmation and inspiration.

Dwight Judy
Garrett-Evangelical Theological Seminary
Evanston, Illinois
Winter, 2013

INTRODUCTION

And how is it that we hear,
each of us, in our own native language?
—Acts 2:8

Thirty students in a college campus ministry undertake a month-long 24/7 prayer ministry. They prepare the walls and floor of a room for recording prayers. The walls fill with prayers from the heart—laments, praises, confessions, global concerns. A sacred space has been created.

• • •

An ecumenical group of women meet monthly to pray for world peace. They walk in prayer on a labyrinth, receive inspiration, and share their hopes together.

• • •

A pastor is sent to close an old downtown church in a declining city. As she guides her congregation with scripture reflection (*lectio divina*) over several months, they receive a vision of opening a Free Store to serve the needs of the community. They are renewed as they serve ten thousand people!

• • •

People flood their urban neighborhoods with invitations to worship and to block parties, asking nothing, offering prayer.

OVER THE PAST thirty years, a quiet revolution has been occurring in Christian life. For some people, a renewal of personal prayer accompanied by the reflective reading of scripture has brought about a new relationship with Jesus and his compelling teachings. Others have felt the mysterious sense of divine presence. Liturgies of anointing and healing have created space for profound encounters of personal reconciliation. People across the age spectrum are recognizing the need for daily prayer.

> The sweeping movement of grace by which the world was created and is sustained is orchestrated by God the Holy Spirit. In God's sovereign freedom, the Holy Spirit stirs where God chooses. Remarkably, the Spirit has selected human life as a privileged place of redemptive activity. In the day-to-day rhythms of our life, the Holy Spirit comes to us with gentle persistence, inviting us to join the wondrous dance of life with God.[1]

Spiritual formation began to emerge in Protestant Christianity as a special focus in the 1980s. At that time, it was not clear whether this field of practice would be a passing movement or would endure. Thirty years later, spiritual formation is here to stay, claiming its own place among other dimensions of congregational life. This approach to Christian living is embraced across the theological divides that all too frequently create disunity among Christians. Spiritual formation has secured a place among other disciplines in the seminary classroom and within congregational life as a means for individual and corporate renewal.

In teaching spiritual formation practices through the years, I have repeatedly witnessed the power of the Holy Spirit in the lives of individuals attracted to these studies. A sustaining image for me in this work has been the distinction in the New Testament between the resurrection appearances of Jesus and the moment of Pentecost reported in the book of Acts. Among retreatants and students I observe that individual encounters with the resurrected Christ are very much with us. People are being touched in surprising ways by experiences with Jesus as they open themselves to scripture. Or they are touched by divine grace through the Holy Spirit in a way that causes them to look at Christianity afresh. These experiences may arise in prayer. They may come in moments of profound grief as a sustaining presence. New visions for lay ministry are awakening. Some individuals answer a call to ordained ministry. All are inspired to live more faithfully in the challenge to love God with all of our heart and soul and mind and strength and our neighbor as ourselves (Matt. 22:37-39; Mark 12:30-31; Luke 10:27).

In the New Testament, many individuals encounter Jesus after his resurrection. Each exchange is unique, but always people receive hope. Today people sense similar touches of divine grace. That grace may initiate a radical life reorientation like Paul's change after his divine encounter on the road to Damascus (Acts 9).

Prior to Paul's experience, many others had encounters with Jesus after the Crucifixion. They were being called one by one to rethink their sense of loss in Jesus' death. In these encounters, the individuals who met Jesus between the time of the Resurrection and the event we call Pentecost received a transcendent, sustaining reality. In the New Testament these individual encounters precede the event we call Pentecost, when several thousand people heard this message of Jesus in a public way. In the Pentecost event reported in Acts 2, several thousand people heard the good news of Jesus in their own language. People speaking the many languages of the ancient world were addressed directly and immediately.

As I witness the ongoing call to individuals to claim the way of Jesus in contemporary times, this hopeful thought inspires me: *when so many individuals are encountering Jesus, can a new Pentecost be far behind?*

The stories in this book serve as witness to many small, "quiet" Pentecosts happening across the church. As denominations struggle to sustain structures that served the church well in past generations, we perhaps focus too much on the big picture of institutional decline and miss the renewal taking place in congregations and other settings.

As You Read These Stories

THE ACCOUNTS OFFERED by this book's contributors can be a resource of spiritual formation practices as implemented at the grass-roots level. "A quiet Pentecost" is abounding! People are being met by God and receiving renewed hope for daily life "in their own language." Whether we speak of the divides of cultural and racial distinctions or the more subtle divisions of age and technology use across the age span, every community contains many subgroups. Spiritual formation practices are particularly malleable to such distinctions, as we will see. At the present time, Pentecost may be manifested as increased numbers of active church members and increased giving—or it may not. Just like witnesses to the original Pentecost, we cannot predict what the Holy Spirit will do among us. We need to be careful not to put material criteria on this time of renewal. "What is born of the flesh is flesh, and what is born of the Spirit is spirit" (John 3:6). While it is tempting to judge our achievements on the basis of the material or fleshly results we can see, this Pentecost is different. This Pentecost may be as simple as single encounters between people that foster reconciliation or as dramatic as a congregation discerning a new focus for community mission. This Pentecost may happen when young adults in college discover the power of a media-free day. Elder adults may find the joy of devoting time to their personal prayer disciplines in unexpected ways.

Two contributors to this book, Marianne Chalstrom and Brenda Buckwell, independently reminded me of the quiet appearance of Jesus to the disciples when they were hiding "behind locked doors" in fear (John 20:19-29). This appearance most closely mirrors what is currently happening in small spiritual formation circles. Frequently, in spite of our fears about church survival or relevance to the world, Jesus appears among us when we listen prayerfully together. He still speaks the same word to these small gatherings: "Peace be with you." And he breathes the Holy Spirit among us. In these stories, you will be amazed at the Spirit coming alive within congregations when invited.

Consider spiritual formation practices as means of evangelism. The general population is not aware of the living tradition of contemplative prayer available in Christianity. Many people have left the Christianity of their childhood, sometimes also leaving their conscious theological and faith development behind as they have departed from congregational life. Some have turned to Buddhism or to yoga in an effort to find sustaining practices of meditation that offer a modicum of inner peace on a daily basis. They have not been taught the rich Christian history of Centering Prayer or of *lectio divina*.[2] The reflective, contemplative aspects of Christianity have been neglected. Some contributors to this book have created spiritual life centers offering workshops, retreats, classes, and events to their communities. They have formed a bridge between Christian practice and missional outreach, as they share faith practices with their broader communities.

This new Pentecost involves teaching people of all ages how to listen prayerfully to others, honoring their unique voice, in a time when discourse has become very boisterous and rude in the media and popular culture. In our media-saturated, sound-bite culture, even small moments of silence are radically countercultural. Such a change of perspective may be greeted with confusion. We will look at the inherent challenges of offering this vision of Christian life.

PUSHING THE PAUSE BUTTON

TEACHING CONTEMPLATIVE PRAYER practices, which nurture personal faith, presents two challenges. First of all, these practices are "nonpractices" in the sense that they call us to pause in our busy lives. These are more about listening than speaking. It takes time for people to learn the art of such a pause. Second, these practices, developed in early Christian monastic settings, only recently have returned to public awareness. We are thus seeking to learn and teach these practices largely "on our own." Most of us in the Protestant traditions do not have the sustained daily rhythms of a Christian monastic community in which to cultivate this heart of God's presence. We are seeking to integrate such practices into family life and active participation in the world.

The gentle presence that we cultivate in spiritual formation practice is described well in Parker Palmer's understanding of a "circle of trust." He contrasts a circle of trust with the circles we ordinarily convene:

> A circle of trust is a group of people who know how to sit quietly "in the woods" with each other and wait for the shy soul to show up. The relationships in such a group are not pushy but patient; they are not confrontational but compassionate; they are filled not with expectations and demands but with abiding faith in the reality of the inner teacher and in each person's capacity to learn from it. The poet Rumi captures the essence of this way of being together: "A circle of lovely, quiet people becomes the ring on my finger."[3]

Does it make a difference if we learn to appreciate one another within our congregations across theological and cultural differences? Today it is essential, not a luxury. I've come to deeply appreciate any practice that puts some space between our quick reactivity and our actions. A few decades ago, such practices were demeaned as self-absorbed navel-gazing. Quite the contrary, such practices are essential to break the imprisonment caused by naming anyone different from ourselves as "enemy." We must examine such attitudes and break their power over us in the name of Jesus' calling to compassion.

CULTIVATING THE MEANS OF GRACE

IN *A PLAIN Account of Christian Perfection,* John Wesley named the aim of Christian life to be growth toward perfection in love. What a high goal! This aim of Christian life calls us to profound love of God and inward reconciliation with the many forces at work within our own hearts, as well as compassionate presence with others. To cultivate this growth in love, Wesley offered practices called *the ordinary means of grace.*[4] We come into the grace of God through

- regular attention to the study of scripture
- public and private prayer
- holy conferencing
- fasting or abstinence, and
- attending the sacraments of the church, particularly Holy Communion.

Wesley wrapped these practices in the ethical requirements to "do good" as much as one can and to "avoid doing evil." Rueben Job's book *Three Simple Rules* has brought renewed appreciation for these core spiritual disciplines. People are reclaiming the practices of *searching the scriptures* and *public prayer* in small-group settings, as well as *private prayer. Holy conferencing* (speaking with others about Christian life) is essential for discernment of congregational decisions, as well as sharing the difficulties and breakthroughs of personal spiritual life. We often speak today of "holy conferencing" as individual and small-group spiritual direction. Searching the scriptures, private and public prayer, and holy conferencing enliven the other means of grace and give us a personal understanding of the rhythms of faith, particularly the rhythm of ongoing renewal, described by Thomas Merton as the "paschal rhythm" of prayer:

There is a "movement" of meditation, expressing the basic "paschal" rhythm of the Christian life, the passage from death to life in Christ. Sometimes prayer, meditation and contemplation are "death"—a kind of descent into our own nothingness, a recognition of helplessness, frustration, infidelity, confusion, ignorance. Note how common this theme is in the Psalms. . . . Then as we determine to face the hard realities of our inner life, as we recognize once again that we need to pray hard and humbly for faith, [God] draws us out of darkness into light—grants us the help we require—if only by giving us more faith to believe that [God] can and will help us in [God's] own time. This is already a sufficient answer.[5]

We need help to grow in our capacity to attend to the troubles of our world as well as our inner challenges. But inundation with bad news on a daily basis can have a severely depressing effect upon us. By giving voice to our personal and global concerns in prayer, we are able to receive insight and clarity of life mission each day.

HOW TO USE THIS BOOK

THE FOLLOWING CHAPTERS, organized around key arenas for spiritual formation ministry, offer both resource and inspiration for you to invite the Holy Spirit into your congregational and community life. The stories create a picture of the quiet Pentecost happening across the church and may give rise to ideas for inviting the Spirit into your own situation. Consider creating a small circle of people who pray and brainstorm together in response to the stories.

Start by designating a spiritual life team, committee, or group. It might be a subgroup of the education work area. It might be the members of an existing prayer team ministry. Whether or not there is a place in your current congregational structure for "spiritual formation," the point is to form a group to read and reflect together on the chapter themes.

- Chapter 1 explores several ways small groups devoted to prayer and other spiritual practices invite the Spirit into community.
- Chapter 2 explores worship as spiritual formation.

- Chapter 3 explores a shift in administrative life toward discernment of God's vision for a congregation.
- Chapter 4 explores applications of spiritual formation in two age-groups—youth and elders.
- Chapter 5 explores a variety of prayer forms, including the prayer labyrinth, Centering Prayer, intentional walks in nature, and contemplative art. Special concerns of women's and men's spiritual life are considered.
- Chapter 6 explores creating a specialized focus in spiritual formation within your congregation. Such a ministry can be compared to leaven in the bread of the body of Christ, the church. Stories of successes and challenges from congregations large and small are presented.
- Chapter 7 returns to the theme of a quiet—or not-so-quiet—Pentecost. The vitality of the ministries reported in the book point to a possible re-visioning of the perceived crisis in the mainline church. God is alive and inspiring people who have made themselves available to listen for such a calling. We are all called to listen for that message of life-giving hope in our hearts and to support one another in bringing such vision into life. That is the body of Christ, which does not disappoint us.
- Chapter 8, "Inviting the Spirit into Your Faith Community," leads you through discussion questions for each of the chapters. It is a guide for starting or strengthening spiritual formation ministry in your own setting. The first set of questions, related to this introduction, helps you (1) to assess current spiritual formation practices within your congregation or community and (2) to set a context of prayer for this work together.

May the Holy Spirit join you frequently in your prayer and reflections.

CHAPTER ONE

Inviting the Spirit into
SMALL GROUPS

*To what should I compare the kingdom of God? It
is like yeast that a woman took and mixed in with
three measures of flour until all of it was leavened.*
—Luke 13:20-21

JANNA BORN LARSEN, interfaith chaplain at a continuing care
retirement community, describes her role as "a community spiritual 'enlovener,' one who ministers in order to love and enliven
others to more fully embrace their own spiritual paths and experience
how their spirituality can gift the community and beyond." Even a
small group of people who practice spiritual disciplines provide leavening to their whole community of faith. Whether we speak of *leavening* or *enlovening*, the place to begin spiritual formation ministries is
with a small group of curious, committed people. Randall Hansen, a
pastor who shares his story later, observes, "Even though only a small
percentage of the members of a local church participate in contemplative prayer classes, their work positively impacts the life of the entire
church. There is a centeredness in the participants that, more often
than not, manifests itself in a nonanxious excitement about their faith
life, which radiates to others in the congregation."

A programmatic focus that begins small can grow into a specialized ministry, such as the Spiritual Life Center of Saint Luke's United
Methodist Church in Indianapolis, which has an e-mail list of two
thousand people, half of whom do not self-identify the congregation
as their church home but are welcome participants in a large array of
retreats, small-group studies, and weekly practices.

The first story witnessing to a quiet Pentecost shows the potential
of a small group to "enloven" their congregation in subtle ways:

A four-week Sunday morning series, "Journey into Prayer," introduced a number of ways our prayer lives could be more richly
developed. Five of us were encouraged to meet the "yearning for God"
in the form of a prayer group. We were advised to simply "start praying."
We envisioned groups of not more than eight people meeting weekly for
one-hour sessions. We described to a list of potential participants what
we thought a contemplative prayer group might look like:

> A group intended for those who are looking for a deeper experi-
> ence of prayer and desiring to make prayer a more powerful
> source of strength in their lives. We are seeking a quiet time
> to set aside for "listening for God," with the accountability
> afforded by a group experience. We are ready to move from
> studying prayer to practice.

Our focus is on each individual deepening his or her relationship
to God rather than acting as a support group. Our chosen method for
each session is the practice of *lectio divina* as outlined in Norvene Vest's
Gathered in the Word, which describes the ancient method of praying the
scripture within small groups. After a short period of "coming together,"
we quiet ourselves by lighting a candle or striking a small Tibetan bowl
to prepare for "hearing the Word." The leader reads a selected scripture
twice, after which members are invited to repeat a word or phrase that
stands out to them. Following the next reading we reflect upon and
share how the phrase has touched them. After a period of silence as
the scripture is read once again, we listen for an invitation of how to
respond to the Word in the coming week. Allowing further time for individual contemplation and having listened to one another's responses,
the group concludes with personal prayers that include a prayer for and
about the person seated on our right.

Leaders have occasionally brought material such as poetry, hymn
verses, or other short readings. Other formats have been introduced,
such as the *examen*, in which we review life experiences looking for
God's presence, but we have primarily stayed close to the *lectio* practice.

The group has provided a context for stimulating both discipline and
new directions in individual contemplation. It has been a private journey
traveled alongside people who have come to love and trust each other.
We have encouraged one another to set time aside for daily devotional
reading and meditation and have learned to pray our gratitude and

concerns aloud even while wrestling with our individual images of the God we are addressing.

While our group itself is not obvious to the congregation, our search for spiritual depth has been recognized and supported by our pastoral staff, and over the past six years classes on spiritual formation have become prominent in adult programming.

Has this quiet group been leaven in the Spirit for this congregation? The growth of spiritual formation offerings suggests that is indeed what has happened.

PRAYING THE SCRIPTURES

LECTIO DIVINA, PRAYING the scriptures, has been a significant part of spiritual formation from early in Christian history, drawing on its roots in the Hebraic tradition:

> Happy are those who do not follow the advice of the wicked,
> or take the path that sinners tread,
>   or sit in the seat of scoffers;
> but their delight is in the law of the LORD,
>   and on his law they meditate day and night.
> They are like trees planted by streams of water,
> which yield their fruit in its season,
>   and their leaves do not wither.
> In all that they do, they prosper. —Psalm 1:1-3

Lectio means "reading"; and *divina,* "holy word." Thus *lectio divina* means reading the holy Word or holy reading. While Christians take scripture seriously, we may not have been taught the simple process of reading scripture, lingering over it, and listening for direct inspiration from the text. Dietrich Bonhoeffer wrote eloquently of our need for daily meditation on scripture: "As a Christian I learn to know Holy Scripture only by hearing sermons and by meditating prayerfully."[1] One of the most powerful ways to learn to pray is to begin with the Bible—reading a few verses, listening for an image or message that speaks directly to us, and then prayerfully seeking to apply it to our lives. We are listening for God's Word or message of inspiration, exhortation, or guidance for our lives.

Marianne Chalstrom describes the power of sustained work with scripture for an ecumenical group of women who explored scripture story through a variety of imaginative processes:

> I developed this class out of years of pastoral experience and frustrated observation that all too often churches succeed at Christianizing people without really moving them toward inward transformation that helps them become more loving and Christlike. Yet it's the latter task that the Gospels attest is possible; the texts themselves carry that power when opened with the imagination (heart) engaged. That has been true in my own life and throughout my ministry.
>
> I invited nine women to my home, representing three churches and two denominations. We were a diverse group, spanning three generations, some lesbian, some straight. This small group had two aims:
>
> 1. teach life-transforming ways of reading the Gospel, inviting participants to engage the imagination in various ways;
>
> 2. build community as we came together to share our experience with the text during the week.
>
> Some questions we hoped to address in the course of this group experience were:
>
> 1. How can reading these familiar texts become new in my experience?
>
> 2. How can scripture reading, the Gospel passages in particular, lead me to new levels of personal growth and healing?
>
> 3. How can reading the Gospel accounts help me be a better follower of Jesus?
>
> Resources I drew upon in writing this course were Morton Kelsey, *The Other Side of Silence;* and John Sanford, *The Kingdom Within.*[2]
>
> I gave participants a list of different ways to read scripture engaging imagination, called "methods of reading the Bible for transformation." Some of these are basic journaling techniques, such as "Write a letter to one of the story participants," or "Imagine yourself as one of the persons in the account and write about it." Some of them are traditional reflection practices such as *lectio divina.* The process was simple: each week we all read the same Gospel text, then reflected on it using the method of our own choosing. The group process was also simple. After a brief invocation asking the Holy Spirit's blessing and guidance, we read the text together to bring it before us, then I opened the conversation with something like "Who has something to share about how this text

impacted your life this week? What method did you use and how did it work for you?" Then we all listened as one by one individuals offered what they were comfortable sharing with the group. People asked questions for clarification or affirmed something they identified with; but doctrine and opinion as such were not part of the conversation.

The power of the experience exceeded our expectations: as people got into reading the Gospels for themselves with open mind and open heart, they began to experience God's presence in new ways. Even more astounding was the sense of community that grew in a short time among previous strangers. As we began sharing life experience on a fairly deep level around these Gospel stories, we learned that what we had in common as women was much deeper and stronger than any differences we had.

This experience has been a great encouragement to me spiritually. My main support has been the other pastor in the group. We would meet and debrief following most of the sessions. In the last session of the group we served Holy Communion together. Her encouragement has been a great support during difficult times.

Marianne Chalstrom's Bible study group experimented with different ways of relating to scripture with profound results. The group also experienced what I have come to expect as normative for shared experiences of *lectio divina*—they created a bond of mutual respect that transcends differences of denomination, theological perspectives, generations, and lifestyles. This is "meeting together in Christ." We will find that this experience is essential to developing spiritual community. It happens when we seek to listen for God's guidance together. When we share our experience from prayer, rather than trying to meet first in doctrinal or theological discussion, trust is created.

This experience of community stands in marked contrast to the fractious ways we meet together in most other places in our culture. We need to be taught how to be "together in Christ." It does not come naturally. We are well equipped to relate to one another from our perceived views of what is right and wrong. Our national political discourse reinforces polarizing viewpoints. Rarely are we taught how to watch over one another in love as the early Methodist societies proposed. By coming together in a prayerful posture and listening for God's message through scripture, community is created. We share in the body of Christ and stand in awe of the unique way each person is being touched and called by God.

TEACHING SPIRITUAL PRACTICES

BETH FENDER, COORDINATOR of New Streams for Illinois Great Rivers Conference of the United Methodist Church, describes the need to teach this kind of sustained spiritual practice within congregations:

Many local churches need help with teaching the basics. In our day, when many of our new members did not grow up in the church and are unaware of much that lifelong church members take for granted, there is a great need for introductory sessions for adults on a variety of topics. Furthermore, since we now have several generations of church members who grew up in an era in which the church valued membership over discipleship, many faithful, lifelong members may be ill-equipped in many of the same spiritual practices. One important topic for both new and lifelong church members is prayer, particularly an introduction to a variety of prayer practices.

Prayer needs to be taught for those who have never attempted the regular discipline of a daily devotional practice, as well as for those who have unsuccessfully attempted such a practice in the past. Many of the church leaders (both laity and clergy) with whom I work have attempted to establish a regular pattern of spiritual practices or daily devotions with varying degrees of success. One does not often rise to leadership in a church without encountering this often unspoken expectation. However, I frequently encounter leaders who express frustration at their seeming inability to sustain the spiritual practices necessary for effective ministry. While there are many reasons for this struggle, three in particular seem to be the most prevalent: a devotional regimen that is incompatible with the leader's personality or stage of spiritual development; a lack of familiarity with various spiritual practices; and a lack of accountability structures to encourage adoption of and long-term commitment to spiritual practices.

Often church leaders have been encouraged by some well-meaning mentor in the past to practice spiritual disciplines that may be a poor fit for their personality. For instance, while journaling is a wonderful tool for spiritual growth, asking someone who thrives on movement and

creativity to spend significant time sitting and writing is unlikely to pro-
duce positive results, even if you provide colored pencils. On the other
hand, this person may enjoy body prayer or liturgical dance—practices
that might frustrate someone who prefers structure or needs to spend
significant amounts of time in silent meditation. Unfortunately, many
people believe that prayer means being seated with hands folded and
head bowed—and must always involve words. With such a mind-set,
it is clear that liturgical dance could not possibly be considered "real"
prayer, and an opportunity for spiritual growth is suppressed or lost.

Other church leaders may have learned to practice certain spiritual
disciplines that worked well for them at an earlier stage in their spiritual
development. Those practices may have worked so well that now the
leader has grown spiritually to the point that new practices are needed
to sustain continued growth.

Rebecca Laird describes challenges that many congregations face
in moving to a deeper level of faith sharing and personal support:

> Several years ago, I was an associate pastor in a large established
> church in the Northeast. One of my tasks was to oversee the
> church's adult spiritual development ministries. We had Bible studies,
> support groups, mission outreach opportunities, and special times and
> services for prayer, but rarely during these ministry gatherings did I hear
> people talk about their life of faith. Talking about community needs,
> social issues, family events, or church politics was easy. Intentional
> conversations about God-at-work in our lives, even in church, almost
> seemed off-limits. The church, with its tall-steeple sanctuary and down-
> town location, attracted members who were characteristically shy about
> God-talk and serious about community service. There were few contexts
> to ask that very Wesleyan question: how is it with your soul?

Randall Hansen regularly leads groups that facilitate deep sharing, as he focuses on contemplative prayer and pastoral care in the
congregations he has served:

> My introduction to "the world behind my eyes" came in the first
> class for my doctor of ministry degree, a class in spiritual dis-
> ciplines. I came to it physically and spiritually exhausted, after nearly
> fourteen years of activist human rights ministry in Latin America as

a United Methodist missionary. I had discovered the hard way Walter Wink's insight that the struggle against evil can bring out the evil in us, both personally and collectively.[3]

Contemplative prayer turned out to be a healing balm for me, and since 1995, I have taught it in each congregation I have served. My modus operandi is, in four sessions, to introduce the theological/biblical foundations of contemplative prayer, the prayer practices of meditation on nature, *lectio divina*, the Jesus Prayer, and Centering Prayer, and then go on to engage some aspect of the faith (reading a book together on the subject) in and through the contemplative prayer practices.

In the churches I have served in the West Michigan Conference of the United Methodist Church, we have explored the labyrinth, ritual and imagery in healing, spirituality and the body, archetypes, dreams, the soul's journey, the interior castle of Teresa of Avila, the parable of the prodigal son, and the quest for the mystical Christ.[4]

After thirty-four years as a parish pastor, during sixteen of which I have offered these classes, I have come to the conclusion that pastoral care and contemplative prayer belong together in the parish. If pastoral care is the attempt "to bring consolation, healing, and compassion to those who suffer without prodding them further into their own [spiritual] journeys," and if spiritual guidance is "the conscious and deliberate attempt to accompany other people on their journeys,"[5] combining pastoral care with contemplative prayer groups allows us to proclaim the healing offered by Christ to individuals and the community of faith in and through our encouraging, equipping, and accompanying people on their journey into God.

I now realize two things: one is that before I offered spiritual guidance through contemplative prayer in the parish, pastoral care ran the risk of being merely palliative—people were consoled, but didn't necessarily grow. The other is that were I to take contemplative prayer out of the parish and offer it without pastoral care, it would run the risk of being esoteric, that is, disconnected from the hurts and challenges of life.

Over the years, I have seen wondrous things happen in the groups. In one, a parishioner with an emotionally broken and physically ailing heart found the peace of Christ, and her healing resulted in the wholeness of her entire family. In another, after years of floundering, a church member discerned her true God-given vocation, and is now actively living out her call. Participants in these groups lead by example, coming forward when we have offered such opportunities for people to grow in their spiritual journey as anointing with oil, laying on of hands, and prayer in Sunday worship.

In my experience, pastoral care and contemplative prayer reinforce each other, making each more effective and thus enhancing the spiritual well-being of the entire congregation.

Rebecca Laird attempted to create such groups within her congregation, but after disappointment with lack of response, she took a different approach. She decided, instead, to add a "faith sharing" component to a women's group already in existence:

For each meeting I selected a first-person story from the local newspaper or a magazine such as *Guideposts* or *Sacred Journey*. Sometimes I used short excerpts from books. The story told of someone's life experience and how they prayed through trouble or saw God at work in everyday life. I would start the group by reading scripture and giving an introduction to the faith theme of the day: praying for enemies, forgiveness, faith in dry periods, faith crises at midlife, praying through chronic illness, cultivating a sense of wonder, etc. Then we would read aloud the first-person story. Each person who was willing would read a paragraph of the article or story as we went around the circle. Then we talked about the story. Little by little people began to relate similar experiences or challenges. We'd end the group with a different style of prayer: silence, the Lord's Prayer, saying when we last felt wonder aloud, or reciting a beautiful prayer from a prayer book. Little by little the sharing increased. One day a woman asked if she could share a story she'd never told anyone but her husband and the group assented. She told a remarkable story of an encounter with God when she was alone and stranded in a snowstorm. We all sat in silent awe after she shared. In the ensuing weeks, we talked less about the lives from the pages of the articles and more about the graces and challenges in our everyday lives.

What Rebecca had created was a circle of trust. When we affirm the power of sharing the stories of our hearts in community, we will discover that "awe" can come "upon everyone" (Acts 2:43).

STARTING COVENANT GROUPS

RICHARD WILSON AT University Park United Methodist Church in Dallas, Texas, describes the evolution of Wesley Covenant Groups, another model of small-group ministry, starting small and growing in influence within the congregation:

Through the vision of several people, two groups were formed in 2000, one of which was exclusively for women. As word spread of the uplifting experiences found in the groups, more groups were formed until we had twenty-four. In 2012, we have sixteen groups, ten for women and six for men, still meeting weekly. Each group meets on a day of the week and time of their choosing. We have groups meeting in the daytime and evening, Sundays through Thursdays. Each meeting is approximately one hour, in which there is a time of gathering and fellowship, a thirty- to forty-five minute time of worship, study, and accountability, a ten- to fifteen-minute time of prayer requests, and a closing prayer.

Each Wesley Covenant Group creates a group covenant that includes sections concerning acts of compassion, justice, worship, devotion, witness to the world, and spiritual guidance. Every group also initiates some form of mission or outreach that members do together.

In the fall of 2011, we conducted a Wesley Covenant Emphasis. This involved one Sunday on which the worship services centered on the work and meaning of Wesley Covenant Groups. Group members wore a button: "Ask Me About WCG." They also stepped up to give testimonials in worship for several weeks prior to the special Sunday, as well as that day and in adult Sunday school classes. We hosted a dinner for people who had joined the church recently and others who desired information about Wesley Covenant Groups. They were invited to form new groups.

Members say that being in such close relationship with others is a blessing for them. Others say that their WCG provides them with accountability, consistency, and support as they grow as Christians. WCG provides an intimate forum for study, discussion, prayer, fellowship, and service as well as renewing spiritual life. Covenant group members participate more in Bible studies, Sunday school classes, Disciple Bible classes [long-term Bible studies], and so forth, and are always ready to assist with the needs of the church when called upon.

This story is testimony to the power of commitment, covenant, and mutual prayer. Notice how small in scale this project and others discussed here began. They did not require large churches or staff. Randall Hansen's work has often been conducted in modest-sized congregations. It requires only a few interested people to start a Wesley Covenant Group.

COMPANIONS IN CHRIST GROUPS

JOANNE KNIGHT OF Christ Church Cathedral (Episcopal) in Nashville relates the significance of Companions in Christ groups led by laity:

There often comes a time in the Christian life when faithful attendance on Sunday morning, singing in the choir, or chairing a committee for an event and participating in outreach is simply not enough for inward significant spiritual growth. There develops a desire for going deeper into an understanding of faith and one's relationship to God that cannot be satisfied by ordinary church life. Few are as fortunate as I was to be in a church that recognized the need and valued spiritual direction for those who wished to go on that path. The church recognized that not all people would be open to this introspective discipline. Only about 25 percent of any congregation is contemplative or even has an interest in the contemplative or introspective, according to Corinne Ware in her book *Discover Your Spiritual Type.* Although I am not by personality type or inclination attracted to contemplative prayer, I was open to new ways of knowing God. If I had to go outside of my comfort zone, I was ready. Fortunately, the need for spiritual growth was acknowledged by our clergy. We had carved out time and space for those who wished to engage in Centering Prayer and had a long tradition of doing so with clergy leadership as well as a history in clergy-led spiritual direction.

The original series required twenty-eight weeks of reading and study, a significant commitment. After the initial series, shorter studies of eight to ten weeks have been developed. Those first participants have grown from six to over seventy, and we add new people every year with a new book or by repeating one. Leadership is generally shared, and in this way everybody grows and has a voice. Meeting times are set by the group; sessions are generally held in the homes of the participants, while some are held at church.

With most new efforts, obstacles stand in the way of success. Some of those obstacles have been the willingness or the unwillingness to be open to the process, being faithful to what is asked of each participant at each meeting, and the understanding and acceptance of moving from informational to formational learning.

But for me it was a little different. When I was first introduced to the Companions series and became familiar with the questions and exercises, I had an initial significant pushback on what I perceived to be somewhat silly questions. I became resistant in general. But since I had committed to honor the process, I continued and was so glad I did, because what I discovered is that formation takes a lot of introspection, and this entails spiritual and psychological work. Answering those questions, doing those exercises, became the vehicle by which I became more self-aware and conscious of who I am authentically and honest in my relationship to Christ—what it is and what it isn't. The process is transformational. The disciplines bring a balance to life, calmness of the spirit, and an awareness of holy listening to others, where there is no need to judge, reform, correct, or recommend. Listening becomes a gift to the speaker and hearer together. So the message could be to the congregation, "Embrace the encouragement to explore other ways of knowing God. After all, you can value your own way and still explore and appreciate other ways."

Here Joanne articulates the difference between *information* and *formation*. Without the practices she describes, we stay at the surface of our spiritual life. With them, we can begin to find new personal depth and transformation promised to us in scripture. The Companions in Christ series carefully guides the process of self-awareness and reflection in a way that fosters sharing of personal and spiritual insights within a small group. Her description follows so well the basic injunction from Teresa of Avila, who said the gateway through which to enter our spiritual life is "prayer and reflection."[6]

SPIRITUAL PRACTICES IN ADMINISTRATIVE GROUPS

IF THESE DISCIPLINES are to enliven or "enloven" congregations, it is important to invite lay and clergy leadership into these practices. Nancy LeValley, lay coordinator of spiritual formation at Traverse Bay United Methodist Church in Traverse City, Michigan, describes her trepidation and amazement at such an invitation:

Ann, the chairwoman of our Administrative Council, requested that I teach a spiritual practice at the beginning of the last four meetings of the year. For several years I've done formative devotions for the group, but this request resulted in some deep discernment. How does one teach spiritual practice in twenty-five to thirty minutes every other month? Spiritual practice does not happen overnight or in hit-and-miss presentations. How would I know the material would even be received, let alone practiced? I wasn't supposed to. If anyone could do it, God could!

I asked Ann what she hoped for or envisioned in changing the format of Administrative Council. Her answer: "I was attempting to provide an opportunity to grow their faith and allow them to be the leaders of not only their work areas but also faith leaders. The real function of Ad Council is to be a forum for ideas that are God-inspired and faith-pursued. We cannot be that type of council unless we are growing in our faith, individually and as a group." Our pastor, Rev. Jane Lippert, and the church staff concurred that this would be a worthwhile effort.

Reading Linda Douty's book *How Can I See the Light When It's So Dark: Journey to a Thankful Heart* I decided if we only developed the discipline of a thankful heart, it could change us all and bring our congregation to a new level. I bought a small spiral notebook for each person in the council to record chronicles of gratitude. The presentation was well received. I summarized several points from the book, read three examples of gratitude from the book, and gave them the assignment of writing down three things every day for which they were thankful until the next session. Later in that meeting one member called for a matter to be brought to prayer on the spot—unusual behavior for that person. It was a holy moment for our council.

Session Two (two months later): Most persons admitted they'd been faithful to their Gratitude Chronicles for a short while, but hardly anyone was continuing the practice. We acknowledged that gratitude is a life-changing force, then changed pace into a body prayer: walking and waiting to the rhythm of favorite hymns. This was hard for some. We took time to identify our prayer styles from Patricia Brown's *Paths to Prayer: Finding Your Own Way to the Presence of God.*

Session Three (two months later): This session included a practice of *lectio divina* and *examen.* Because our regular meeting space was unavailable, we met in a room next to a nursery full of happy, noisy children. I gulped and began reading the assigned passage from Exodus. A colleague said quietly, "Slow down, Nancy." I stopped abruptly, realizing what was happening, and invited everyone into prayer. Peace settled over all of us. The noise level didn't change, but it was no longer a distraction. What an eye-opener! It was God who was in charge and wanted to grow us!

Session Four (two months later): We revisited *examen* by using the November Spiritual Tools from *Alive Now.* The challenge was to examine the best thing that had happened to us individually that day, then the worst thing.[7] We then had a time of sharing with one other person. I was amazed to hear and see lots of sharing. We briefly evaluated the previous four sessions, mentioning practices that were especially meaningful.

This was a successful experiment—not because everyone had absorbed every part of our journey, but because all had appreciated the experiences. We have been invited to continue this process by the next chairperson of the council. I learned that smaller bites of information and practice might be helpful in the future.

BECOMING A CONGREGATION OF SOUL FRIENDS

WHAT DOES THE church of the future look like? The changes at Central Presbyterian Church in Lafayette, Indiana, may give us a glimpse. Jeff Cover shares an account of how years of spiritual formation work have affected life there:

We encourage spiritual life at Central Presbyterian Church in many ways. Each year our adult discipleship team ensures that there are short-term spiritual formation options in its adult education program, classes such as "Prayer and Temperament," "Discernment," and

"Sharing Your Faith Journeys." Lenten studies focus on spiritual themes, among them a review of the five stages of spiritual growth gleaned from Evelyn Underhill's *Mysticism*, a study of the WellSpring resource *How to Eat Your Bible*, and introducing such practices as *lectio divina* and Ignatian exercises for entering imaginatively into scripture. Deborah Cover, trained in spiritual formation at Columbia Theological Seminary, has led once-a-year off-site retreats on topics like "Finding God in the Everyday" and "Discernment: Listening to God in Times of Choice." Central's Women of the Word and Koinonia study groups offer several Bible and book studies each year. As associate pastor I have also helped to organize community-wide ecumenical monthly worship services in the meditative style of Taizé.

Using funds from a Clergy Renewal grant from the Lilly Endowment, the church is having a "Year of Spiritual Exploration." We have invited three highly regarded speakers to teach and to preach for the congregation. Marjorie Thompson, author of several books in the Companions in Christ series; Rodger Nishioka, professor of Christian education at Columbia Theological Seminary; and J. Phillip Newell, former warden at the Iona Community in Scotland, will all come to Central. We hope these diverse speakers will convey to the larger congregation that there are different ways of being spiritual and will encourage a wider range of members to deepen their prayer lives.

The mainstay of spiritual formation, though, is the monthly *Anamchara* (Celtic term for "soul friends") spirituality group. Each month I lead the group in exploring an aspect of spiritual life and then suggesting a prayer practice that fits the theme. Among our themes have been spiritual friendship, the desert fathers and mothers, spiritual autobiography, sacred places, spiritual resources for public life, Benedictine spirituality, and seasonal spirituality. We have explored Jewish *beracha* (daily blessings), praying the Psalms, Native American spirituality, *The Cloud of Unknowing*, meditation, and developing a rule of life. We have also worked with dialogical prayer, breath prayer, body prayer, the Lord's Prayer, prayer and personality, spiritual guidance and friendship, forgiveness, contemplation, and intercessory prayer. We have worked with material from Thomas Merton, Hildegard of Bingen, John Calvin, and Teresa of Avila.

The Anamchara group has been meeting for four years now. New people are welcomed during our January–March open enrollment each year. While some have come and gone, participation has been remarkably steady. Participants report that the group has enriched their prayer lives and given them a vocabulary with which to speak of things dimly sensed but deeply felt. They often speak of connections they are making with their daily lives and how they are learning to carve out times for conversation with God. We look forward to the encouragement we receive from one another, and I find that the group often helps to sustain me in my ministry.

I have used prayer practices introduced to me by Marjorie Thompson; Richard Foster's video resources based on *The Celebration of Discipline* and *Longing for God* (coauthored with Gayle Beebe); and J. Phillip Newell's *Listening for the Heartbeat of God: A Celtic Spirituality*.

We pray together at each Anamchara meeting and often pray for one another between meetings. Knowing with others we are in prayer makes us more accountable in our spiritual lives.

In the process of meeting together and discussing the challenges and joys of being praying persons, our conversation has grown deeper and our relationships with God more sustaining. Sometimes it has been an uphill battle to acquaint the larger congregation with the available resources our faith has for discerning God's guidance. We long for others in the congregation to come to know deeper spiritual intimacy with Jesus Christ and with each other.

As individuals share their prayer experiences with one another, they are "enlovened" and discover the body of Christ in their midst. This chapter has introduced groups using *lectio divina*, Wesley Covenant focus, faith sharing, and Companions in Christ resources, as well as customized spiritual formation programs. Imagine your congregation steeped in prayer, bathed in mutual respect and love for one another, enlovening each other with God's grace. In the following chapters we will continue to explore how spiritual formation with a focus on the disciplines of personal prayer, reflection on life challenges, corporate worship, meaningful administrative structures, and vision for various ministries within the community can invite the spirit into our midst. Is this the "new life" for which the church is longing? "Come and see" (John 1:46).

CHAPTER TWO

Inviting the Spirit into
WORSHIP

Praise the LORD!
Praise God in his sanctuary;
praise him in his mighty firmament!
Praise him for his mighty deeds;
praise him according to his surpassing greatness!

Praise him with trumpet sound;
praise him with lute and harp!
Praise him with tambourine and dance;
praise him with strings and pipe!
Praise him with clanging cymbals;
praise him with loud clashing cymbals!
Let everything that breathes praise the LORD!
Praise the LORD!
—Psalm 150

FOR SOME YEARS churches have been caught in the debate over classical forms of worship versus those built around contemporary praise music. This may have blunted the real question: *does our worship take us out of ourselves into praise of God?* Does it enable us to reflect on God's redeeming work and invite us to pray for all the pain of the world? Is there opportunity for praise, confession, reflection on scripture, silence, and invitation to new life?

Spiritual formation practitioners are exploring new ways of approaching worship as the primary venue for spiritual formation of the congregation. As they do so, they are finding ways to integrate ancient practices with a variety of contemporary forms. We are invited to worship God in praise, in music, in sounds of cymbals, and with the awe expressed in silence.

Spiritual formation and contemplative prayer practices, like reflective reading of scripture, enable us to slow the pace of our busy minds and lives. Without reflective moments, our minds race along, captured by the most recent trend or product. It's astonishing how many words and images we encounter each day, all competing for our attention. It is more important than ever to find time when we may be called into praise and hope for victory over life's challenges. We receive this gift in worship with others. Worship invites us into reflection on our own life through scripture, exhortation of the Word, prayers, hymns, and support of the community. We emerge refreshed and ready for the week ahead.

In teaching forms of prayer, I point to two primary categories—*active prayer* and *dispositional prayer*. I came upon these terms many years ago in the book *Don't You Belong to Me?* written by Father Paul Konkler, "a Monk of New Clairvaux," a Trappist monastic community in California. The term *active prayer* describes those prayer forms in which we, as human beings, address our concerns to God, for example, intercession, petition, and confession. We are the actor, the agent of the conversation; God is the recipient of our requests. *Dispositional prayer* refers to those forms of prayer in which we engage our minds only a little so that we can dispose ourselves to listen for God. God is the actor, the agent of the conversation. We seek to listen for guidance. Such prayer forms are ordinarily described as contemplative and are the foundation of the spiritual disciplines. Other forms of Christian prayer through the centuries have included the Jesus Prayer, chanting the Psalms, the prayer labyrinth, and Centering Prayer. We are witnessing a renaissance of prayer forms that work in both active and dispositional ways. We will learn more about the variety of prayer forms in chapter 5.

When we apply these two terms to worship, we need to ask if there is adequate opportunity for both active and dispositional prayer within our time of worship. Do the prayers of the people enable us to pray for the concerns of the whole world, actively giving voice to our social, ecological, and political concerns? Do we focus only on the health concerns of a few of our congregation? Is there adequate opportunity for us to listen for God and respond? Protestant worship, with its high regard for the preached Word, places great emphasis on the conveyance of God's message through the preacher to the congregation. But does the message touch our hearts? Is there a way to learn from the practice of dispositional prayer how to reach each person, so that every Sunday, "we hear [God's Word], each of us, in our own native language" (Acts 2:8)? Does the experience of worship give adequate space for silence, for the opportunity to receive and reflect on the message? Or do we find ourselves flooded with more and more words and images without the opportunity to reflect? Many congregations use projected visual images and video clips along with the spoken message. These can be wonderful tools to enable the message to come alive, or they can be yet more images flooding our minds so that we don't find our hearts touched. As we apply spiritual formation practices to worship, we discover the power of sensory-rich worship, silence, and symbolic images to invite us into God's presence. Are we allowing ourselves to be opened up, so that the God of transcendence can break through? Are we so busy keeping up with a great onslaught of words and images that there is no space for the holy moment?

Barbara Holmes describes a breakthrough in an African American congregation:

> The soloist moves toward the center of the podium. The congregation of about 1,500 breathes with her as she moans "Oh . . . oh . . . oh, Jesus." Those are the only words to the song. Unless you are sitting within the sound of her voice, it is difficult to imagine how a song of two words can be a cry of anguish, balm, and celebration. In each soaring note we participate in the unutterable spectrum of human striving. In this world you will have trouble but—"oh, oh, oh, Jesus." The shouts of exaltation give no indication of what is happening. Although it appears to be the usual charismatic congregational fare, in fact we are riding the stanzas through time to the hush arbors and swamp meetings, over the dangerous waters to safety. In this ordinary Sunday service something has happened and we are changed. The worldly resistance to transcendence that we wore into the sanctuary has cracked open, and the contemplative moment carries us toward the very source of our being.[1]

Several years ago Rev. Leroy Cothran, pastor of United Mission-ary Baptist Church in Dayton, Ohio, was introduced to contemplative prayer practices. Shortly after he began practicing holy listening, he was inspired to observe a moment of silence at the beginning of each worship service. After the choir opened the service, he invited the congregation to be silent before God. This silence provided an oppor-tunity for God to "crack open" worldly resistance to transcendence. Many contemporary praise band music leaders have discovered the power of juxtaposing rhythmic, joyful praise with quieter songs that invite congregants into a time of personal reflection. Our only appro-priate response to a true encounter with God is to allow our minds to be silent.

SENSORY-RICH WORSHIP

ONE WAY TO influence the worship life of a congregation is to invite people into a new style of worship, perhaps at a different time of the week than other occasions for worship in your congregation. Suzanne Clement describes her work with Evening Prayer and Eucharist:

> Darkness begins to settle, and the shadows cast from dozens of flickering candles create a shadow dance on the walls of the dimly lit sanctuary. The profile of the cross, backlit to dramatic effect, calls us to lift our eyes and turn our minds toward Christ. The aroma of freshly baked bread permeates the air we breathe in anticipation of the meal we will share. The faithful who are called to this discipline enter and gather in silence, each immersed in his or her thoughts. Taizé music plays softly in the background.
>
> At the hour, the chime calls us into awareness of our oneness within this group and with the whole church as we share in the timeless rhythm and practice of Evening Prayer and Eucharist. The vesper candle is lit and the leader intones, "Light and peace in Jesus Christ," and the response is chanted, "Thanks be to God."
>
> Thanks be to God indeed for the gift of Evening Prayer, in which we join our prayers with those of the whole body of Christ in unceasing prayer and praise to the one who made us. We settle into the rhythm of song and prayer, intercessions, scripture, and silence that I have come to understand as story and relationship. Through those simple means

we affirm who God is and who we are in relationship with the Holy One. We share the stories of our faith, stories of God's faithfulness and active presence in the lives of his children throughout many centuries. Hearts open and thoughts soar as we settle deeper into the mystery, "Deep calls to deep at the thunder of your cataracts" (Ps. 42:7). The intercessions, sharing of present hopes and troubles, and lifting prayers for others bring into sharp focus just how much we need that relationship with the Father, the Son, and the Holy Spirit; we are aligned with the reality of God active and present, here and now. A deeper knowing assures us that the God who was and is, is also the God who will be always and forever real in our lives.

In that consciousness we reenact the meal that binds us together as the body of Christ, open to all who would come and partake in peace and harmony and love with brothers and sisters, then are sent forth to share what we have been given through the self-emptying, sacrificial love of the Savior.

Our practice of Evening Prayer was conceived in a series of Wednesday-afternoon conversations I had undertaken along with another friend and our associate pastor to define spiritual formation ministry in our church. Our congregation had been experiencing some difficulties as a result of leadership changes and seemed to be languishing in some sort of congregational depression. My friend and I had grown to love the rhythm of daily prayers we had experienced as participants in the Upper Room Two-Year Academy for Spiritual Formation, and on that score the three of us were of one accord. We decided to feature a series of Evening Prayer services for Advent that year and believed that there might be enough interest to sustain it for the season. Our associate pastor agreed to celebrate the Eucharist each week, and I was to plan the actual service. It was with no small amount of anxiety that I prepared for the first service. The liturgies for evening prayer, "Celebration of Word and Table," and healing prayers from the *Upper Room Worshipbook* were combined; scriptures selected; and the sanctuary prepared. What if no one came?

What if sixty-five people came? That is what happened, and attendance stayed high through Advent and on through Lent. The forms eventually changed, attendance changed; but for me there was never a question that what was happening was important. Healing took place the more we prayed together and shared Holy Communion. We began to notice that Bible studies and study groups filled more easily. I will always believe that those prayers and the weekly Eucharist sustained our congregation through some very difficult times. When participation dropped to near nothing, I kept on, because God would not let me stop. I never sat or prayed alone; always someone would come who needed respite, who needed prayer and healing and to talk. It became a spiritual direction time for a few. Intentionality in designing the services is required. I plan everything that goes on in the time we spend together. My approach has been for the work of design to be a practice of devotion. Everything included is intended to evoke awareness of the Spirit. Each element should evoke and invite us into some form of contemplation of meaning. Every act provokes and pushes us toward transformation and changed behavior.

The point of any practice geared toward spiritual formation is transformation, to become fully what God intended us to be, Christlike. Orders of worship can be adjusted; forms can change, but our journey together in community is still sharing story, sharing hopes, dreams, struggles, holding one another in prayer, bearing with one another, studying, working, and serving together in the name of Jesus Christ.

"The wind blows where it chooses, and you hear the sound of it, but you do not know where it comes from or where it goes. So it is with everyone who is born of the Spirit" (John 3:8). Suzanne Clement describes a ministry in which the Holy Spirit is truly present. She shows the kind of flexibility necessary for such initiatives. She is both careful in the discernment of the initial venture and faithful to her own sense of divine calling.

Mercy Center, a Sisters of Mercy convent and retreat center in Burlingame, California, has provided a monthly Taizé service for the community for more than two decades. Upon entering the chapel for the first time, I was amazed to find myself with several hundred people in a setting of exquisite beauty. The chapel lights had been dimmed; the cross on the floor was outlined by candles. Simple chants, the reading of scripture, and times of silence and prayer were offered. Persons could kneel at the cross to offer their prayers and petitions. We must ask ourselves if we form each service of worship with such care.

In the services of Evening Prayer and Eucharist and the Taizé service at Mercy Center, we note great attention to the worship center, to symbolic expressions like the cross and candles, and to the senses. Worship may be the primary place we receive the opportunity to reflect upon our lives through rich symbols that are poignant expressions of Christian life. The cross, candles, banners, altar cloths determined by liturgical season all reflect "the old, old story of Jesus and his love." These elements are not nostalgic but evoke the long history of people seeking to make sense of their life journeys.

I present a retreat called "Sacred Story, Our Story," intended to help individuals discover that each of their life stories is as rich in confusion, wonder, and meaning as the stories in the Bible. The more we steep ourselves in the rich stories of scripture, the more they become archetypal patterns that enable us to make sense of our own life stories. When we find ourselves lost in rage over wrongs inflicted or in grief, the Psalms give voice to our deep longings. When we find ourselves summoned to journey into unknown places, we can take heart from Abram and Sarai, who were called to leave their home (Gen. 12). When we "walk through the valley of the shadow of death," we look for the comfort of the divine "rod" and "staff" to guide us (Ps. 23). Symbols embedded in sacred stories can come alive if we think about a primary image within each scripture that shapes the sermon, the music, and all other aspects of worship. That takes intentionality and prayer. It takes a sense of dwelling with the scripture to discern a theme around which to shape the worship experience. As we practice *lectio divina* in our own devotional life, we learn to listen for a key image, symbol, or metaphor to arise. We can practice the same discipline by reflecting on the scriptures before a service of worship or liturgical season.

Nancy Dibelius describes how to establish a focal point for worship that is rich in symbolism. She explains how to develop a particular theme and then bring it to life in a symbolic way. This process can be used for specific events or retreats, as well as for developing the worship theme. The process works in a conference room or a sanctuary:

> The first step in designing worship is to explore and understand a theme; find a way to incorporate the theme into your own rhythm of life and prayer. Before you can invite others into a space where the

experience becomes real, it must first be real for you and your journey. If you are developing a retreat or special event, have a clear theme. If you are developing a worship center for corporate worship, work with the pastor and worship team to understand the theme for worship. If there are key ideas for the sermon or prayers or hymns already developed, work with these, as well. As you think on these themes or the scriptures for worship, choose one or two focal ideas that uniquely embody the theme for you and let these become part of your daily rhythm of prayer and reflection. Once you have lived with the theme for a while, lift up your experiences in prayer.

Once you have chosen a scripture, read through it several times; in your imagination, what do you see, what do you hear, what do you smell, what is there to touch? Make a list of these things and then go back to the scripture, hymns, and prayers, looking for additional sights and sounds and add them to your list. Has some clear visual emerged? Consider the space in which you will be worshiping. How do you transform that space so that it is inviting and becomes holy space for others? After you have a sense for the way in which you wish to transform the room, think about how to accomplish it. See the image in your mind. Consider everyday materials that could be used to turn the vision into reality. Start your own collection of what I refer to as "holy hardware"—fabric, candles, candle-holders, crosses, pitchers, bowls, stones, worship-related objects, etc. If you are doing this for the first time, try it out. Find a place similar in size to the space you will be using and actually lay out the room as you have imagined it. Walk around in it and rehearse what will happen there. When you are satisfied, draw a sketch or take a photograph, make a list of the materials you have used, and be sure you can reproduce it easily.

Now that you have a visual for the room, consider details. If you are using an altar, how will you design a worship center for the altar? How will you coordinate the altar with the larger visual for the room? Consider colors, texture, objects that will represent key symbols, sounds, smells, and things to touch. Don't overdo; sometimes less is more. If you end up with too many symbols, congregants will not focus on the key symbol; they will be distracted. Be sure that you understand why you are using a specific symbol.

Stacey Gassman describes how these elements come together through the use of art in a United Church of Christ sanctuary during

Lent and Easter. She explains how to give worshipers a fresh perspective of the sanctuary. Stacey draws in images inspired by scripture, nature, and urban streets:

When working on an art piece for worship, two major considerations are the environment and the thematic elements. Every worship space has a different personality. Listen to what the space has to offer: view it from many different angles and positions—from the chancel, from the choir loft or balcony, from the front row of pews, and the back. Get a feel for the architecture itself: Is it ornate woodwork and plaster columns? modern? Is your sanctuary long and rectangular or more circular and wide? Are there devices installed that might be helpful such as pulley and wires, banner hangers, pipes, or other technical elements that might be of use? And consider the theme—what do you want to say? Why are you installing art now? Is it because of a particular season or a particular worship service? What medium will you be working with and what resources are available?

I first had the idea to bring an art installation into a church I was serving during Lent. Lent is a time of deep reflection and penitence, a time in the desert to simplify and look deep within. Lent is a journey that leads toward the Cross. One symbol to which I have always responded deeply is light from a candle. In our technology-filled twenty-first-century lives, a candle flame focuses us, makes us slow down and remember a time before instant messaging and television programs on-demand. The color of the season of Lent is purple, signifying penitence and royalty. Given these reflections, I wanted to have certain elements as part of the installation: candles, the color purple, and the colors of the desert, and stones signifying simplicity and connection with the earth and our ancestors who lived closer to it. A major architectural element of the space I was working with was the steps leading to the chancel area. The rise made an excellent focal point.

As I studied the space, the image of a cross made with candles, stones, and purple fabric cascading down the chancel stairs emerged. Experimenting is an important and necessary part of the process. I began by laying the elements out and realized that the rise of the stairs was too dramatic. In order to even out the fall of the cross, I used spare hymnals under the fabric, layering the candles and stones on top. This is an example of a simple temporary installation that offered a dramatic and centering effect and served as point of focus during worship. I modified the cascading cross for Easter, using white fabric draped across the organ screen and down the chancel stairs. Pink blossoms and palm leaves added visual interest and a sense of celebration.

Preparing our worship spaces carefully is important. Images can create an atmosphere for prayer and contemplation. It is equally important to consider the people who will be attending the service, particularly individuals with various limitations or disabilities.

WORSHIP WITH MEMORY-IMPAIRED ADULTS

WORSHIPING WEEK AFTER week, year after year, through stories, liturgies, and symbols, embeds these elements deep in our souls. Janet Aldrich, a chaplain at a retirement center, describes how images like those described in Stacey's story above can help individuals to continue to "be themselves" in worship, even if dementia has impaired their memory. She designed liturgies based upon extensive research regarding the capacities of memory-impaired individuals:

> Corporate worship is "first and last, praising, giving thanks, and blessing God."[2] I contend that we must bring the vibrancy of color, texture, sound, and movement into praise and worship. Sensory-rich worship opens us to the deeper mysteries of faith and life. Worship liturgy for memory-impaired residents should incorporate "old" hymns, familiar prayers and scripture, and other symbols of faith that are deeply embedded in long-term memory.[3] Although memory-impaired individuals may have difficulty communicating with others, we should begin our worship preparation with the belief that all of us possess a core of being that we sometimes call the soul. "At the deepest level of human existence, deeper than intellect and personality which are debilitated by the disease and outwardly less approachable by human means, the inward spirit, the God-breathed life remains."[4] Include memory-impaired individuals in the worshiping community whether or not they seem to be "aware" of what is going on around them. We can never know what will trigger their memory of God at any given moment—symbols of water, bread, wine, oil, light, the chapel setting, a familiar hymn, a gentle soothing touch, a clerical collar, a cross. Only God knows.[5]

For my doctoral project, I created a worship series for memory-impaired residents living in a long-term continuing care retirement community. The series followed the liturgical calendar and used visual arts (colors, objects or symbols, fabrics or banners), familiar music, and simple movement as well as words to enable wider avenues of participation for the residents. I witnessed firsthand that the special worship services offered comfort, meaning, and a sense of peace to the residents. I felt the power of the Holy Spirit in our midst. It is my hope that other clergy ministering to memory-impaired older adults will be open to the transformation of the Holy Spirit and reach out to these persons so that all of God's children may continue to hear the good news of Jesus Christ. God holds their memories for them, and God never forgets.

Janet Aldrich's work with memory-impaired older adults points us toward the power of images, music, and symbolic expressions to convey the divine mystery. Some profound images I have experienced in worship recently include (1) family members of a deceased loved one leading the procession during All Saints' Day worship, holding lighted candles and placing them on the altar; (2) pastors walking infants into the congregation at baptism, allowing me the opportunity to prayerfully offer my grown sons to God at this stage of their life journey; (3) a large rugged cross on which people are encouraged to nail their confessions during Lent, with each nail removed in prayer before Easter Sunday worship; (4) wedding vows voiced with an invitation for those in attendance to renew their own wedding vows. Frequently we hear appreciation for children's sermons because they grasp us in simple, symbolic ways. One of the most profound I've witnessed was on the Sunday preceding the Martin Luther King Jr. holiday. At First United Methodist Church in Evanston, Illinois, Pastor Dean Francis ushered thirty or more children into the imposing pulpit, then explained that Dr. King had preached in that pulpit before his death. He summoned the whole congregation to be a witness for social justice.

HEALING PRAYER IN WORSHIP

A FEW YEARS ago I was invited to preach at an Ash Wednesday service. In addition to the imposition of ashes, worship leaders invited congregants to stay at the altar rail for healing prayer. Out of approximately three hundred people in attendance, at least seventy came to one of the four prayer stations. The acts of asking, receiving, touching, and anointing are opportunities for God's grace. Attentiveness to the symbolic power of such actions deepens our awareness of God's presence. Lowell Black describes the formation of a similar prayer ministry at First United Methodist Church in Valparaiso, Indiana:

> Mindy Ohler was a San Francisco firefighter who died in the line of duty. Her parents, members of our church in Indiana, wanted to have some sort of lasting legacy to memorialize her life of service to others. The idea to establish a healing altar in our church arose.
>
> The altar itself is built as a side altar in the main sanctuary. Mindy's father hand-carved the wooden wall hangings for the three walls around the altar itself. He also embroidered the cushion for the kneeler.
>
> In preparation for the dedication of the altar, the senior pastor conducted a class on healing prayer. Several members of the congregation participated, creating a core cadre of laity to provide healing prayer at the altar. Healing prayer is offered each time Holy Communion is observed.
>
> The concept was entirely new for our congregation and we were curious to see what would happen the first Sunday that Holy Communion was celebrated. The senior pastor explained the function of the altar as a part of the liturgy. As Communion servers took their places, the senior pastor and one layperson took position at the healing altar. The number of people who came to avail themselves of the healing presence of God exceeded our expectations.
>
> We continue to offer prayer at the altar each time we celebrate Holy Communion. I encourage others to learn more about healing prayer. Services of healing can be a time of great interaction between the congregation and God.
>
> God is still present today in answering our prayers, and this altar is no exception to that premise. I often tell people that God always answers our prayers—sometimes yes, sometimes no, sometimes not now. Sometimes the best we can do is ask for God's peace in a situation. And other times we simply cry out in our prayers in solidarity with those suffering. But we always know that God is faithful in answering our prayers as we continue praying for those in need.

TEACHING SPIRITUAL DISCIPLINES IN WORSHIP

PASTORS AND LAY leaders are thinking creatively about how to impact the whole congregation through worship. Because worship is the primary place individuals gather in churches, sermons and scripture are both effective means by which to cultivate a new spirit of listening for God's guidance within a congregation. Sheryl Palmer describes her approach to a churchwide intergenerational sermon series on prayer and its results within her congregation:

At the end of a class on the spiritual disciplines in my doctor of ministry program, I returned to church fired up and ready to find ways to introduce some of these wonderful practices to the people of Saint John's United Methodist Church in Edwardsville, Illinois. While few of the prayer practices were new to me, they were introduced in such a powerful way I could not help but share them with those I was called to serve and lead.

I suspected that some in the congregation were familiar with and practicing these disciplines, but certainly not all. I sensed a hunger among some to delve deeper into their spiritual lives and strengthen their relationship with God.

I used a fourteen-week experiential summer sermon series developed by a fellow student in my doctor of ministry program and supplemented the series with *Habits of a Child's Heart: Raising Your Kids with the Spiritual Disciplines* by Valerie E. Hess and Marti Watson Garlett. I also drew on Adele Ahlberg Calhoun's *Spiritual Disciplines Handbook: Practices That Transform Us;* and Marjorie J. Thompson's *Soul Feast* for various ideas and practices.

Before I knew it, a fourteen-week experiential summer sermon series had turned into an equally experiential summer children and youth Sunday school and children's church program. The series, "Hearing God's Heartbeat," took all involved on an amazing journey of spiritual exploration and growth.

Each Sunday I introduced a new spiritual discipline to the congregation and devoted time to practice it during the sermon whenever possible. For example, in the sermon on fasting, congregants were encouraged to write on a sticky note something they could and would give up to help them draw closer to God. We did a similar exercise when we talked about simplicity. Each week in our newsletter and on our website we provided additional ideas for continued practice of each discipline.

We experienced unprecedented summer worship and Sunday school attendance throughout the series. The energy, excitement, and joy were palpable and contagious throughout the entire summer, and beyond. At the end of the summer, we encouraged congregants to commit to two or three practices that best helped them connect their heart with God. Many are still doing their best to make these practices and disciplines a regular part of their busy but faithful lives.

James Denton is associate pastor of a congregation that has suffered major disruption in recent years and has few adult education opportunities. Here he outlines his approach to spiritual renewal within his congregation through worship and teaching prayer practices within existing groups. He believes that by working from the ground up, people will be more attentive in worship and the spirit of the congregation revived. Though there are few adult education groups with which he might work directly, there are significant numbers of people in the youth group and in the music ministry. On any given Sunday, almost a quarter of those who attend worship are in one of these groups. Denton writes:

In her book *Soul Feast*, Marjorie Thompson emphasizes the importance of private worship for the revitalization of public worship. Daily prayerful scripture reading "becomes tilled soil for receiving the seed of God's Word in the liturgy."[6] The private worship and devotional practices of the congregation form the spiritual basis for heart worship. These practices are introduced to the key groups, including the youth group and choirs. Instruction in *lectio divina* is offered to help facilitate this. Key to this instruction is the idea of using scripture for a holy encounter with God. I suggest the lectionary reading for the upcoming Sunday's sermon be used to help connect this devotional prayer with the public worship of the church. The small groups will begin to bring their developing spirituality into the sanctuary as they gain experience in prayer and grow in fellowship with one another.

Sermons will begin to relate scripture to the love of God and the love of neighbor implicitly. Out of this consistent theme, examples of the fourfold way of Wesleyan discipleship, acts of justice, mercy, devotion, and worship, will be woven into the messages. The purpose of this is to lift up the life of discipleship as the goal of Christian living.

A weekly worship note should be included in the bulletin to explain worship practices, offer suggestions for ways to worship, and guidance for remaining prayerful during those times in worship when we find ourselves less engaged by the words and actions of the services.

Because salvation in the Wesleyn context is about restoring the *imago dei* in each individual, congregations may wish to add a healing component to their worship services, for example, offering a quarterly service of anointing. All worship can be deeply healing. True worship helps people remember the great God before whom we bow in awe, confess our sin, reflect on our own life story in light of the promises of Christ, and pray for all of creation and human suffering. We can be drawn by sensory-rich worship into the great images of faith. We are refreshed, indeed, redeemed in this moment by the peace of right relationships within our community and the world around us. Healing and wholeness can set our feet once again upon the pathway of life.

CHAPTER THREE

Inviting the Spirit into
MISSION DISCERNMENT

*What good is it, my brothers and sisters, if you say
you have faith but do not have works? Can faith save
you? If a brother or sister is naked and lacks daily
food, and one of you says to them, "Go in peace; keep
warm and eat your fill," and yet you do not supply
their bodily needs, what is the good of that? So faith
by itself, if it has no works, is dead.*
—James 2:14-17

CONGREGATIONS CAN LEARN to listen together for God's direction as they seek their mission. The gripping story of renewal from Brenda Buckwell shows us the power of inviting the Spirit into the process of discernment through the practice of *lectio divina,* or prayerful scripture reading.

DISCERNING MISSION THROUGH *LECTIO DIVINA*

I was astonished. The leadership team of the small urban congregation had just signed their death certificate. In response to the question "What is your greatest desire in ministry?" a tenderhearted gentleman in his early seventies, with head held high, stated, "To keep the doors of the church open until the oldest generation dies." The team was not surprised by the man's response. The church had tried various approaches over the years. With one glance at the declining community around the church building, anyone could see the marks of hopelessness and poverty. The closed stores, folks walking rather than driving from one place to another, children running in the streets on school days, drug dealers standing on the corner: all spoke of despair. There seemed to be little opportunity for church renewal and revitalization.

Not surprisingly, however, God had other plans for this aging urban community of believers.

In my astonishment, I paused a moment and then leveled the playing field of mission and ministry for this congregation. With a deep breath and the infilling of the Spirit, I replied: "You can certainly do that if you would like. I can speak to the bishop about sending someone here to your declining ministry to do just that, close the congregation. I am just not that pastor. If you would like to venture forth with me, we can discover God's desire and mission for this congregation together." Now it was the team's turn to be surprised. That very night the leadership team had their first experience of *lectio divina*, and the journey to amazing new life began at First United Methodist Church in Zanesville, Ohio.

Opening the Bible for a prayerful soaking in the Word, I posed questions to the leadership team based on the historical practice of *lectio divina*.[1] In choosing scriptures for vision planning for a church, I work from the perspective that to be vital, the congregation—any congregation—must seek the presence of God's Holy Spirit as the first-century church did. I began with a healing story so they could picture God desiring healing for them. Later, I used the scripture of Jesus walking on water and asking Peter to step out of the boat to develop their capacity for acting on faith. The final scripture was the Pentecost story from Acts 2. After the scripture passage was read, each member responded to the question "What word or phrase catches your attention from this text?" Next, elaborating on the answer a bit more, the conversation grew as they responded to "How does this text intersect with this leadership team for the congregation?" And finally, because we believe that God's Word is a living Word, not just a historical document, we deepened our prayer through invitation. Prior to the third reading of the scripture, I encouraged each person to be open to a third question: "From this scripture, what is God inviting this leadership team to, for the sake of the mission of this congregation?" I recorded the responses and read them back to the community for clarification and accuracy.

After recording each response from the question of invitation, I explained the final step in this community process of praying the scriptures. Confirming that the leaders knew the name of the person on their right, I asked them to pray for one another and the invitations each had heard in the scripture. Audibly each person spoke prayers around the circle. Not just any prayer but a prayer of empowerment for the team and the congregation to live into the invitation stated by the neighbor on the right. As we audibly prayed the other's invitation, no one could insist "my way is the best way" or "I have the perfect direction from God." Each listened to the other's heart's desire and cared for the other's invitation to bear fruit. In that instant God began binding prayer-filled hearts together. New community was born. This praying for one another's invitation is vital to the discovery process that is discernment.

Our discernment journey continued as we prayed the scriptures out loud and set aside personal agendas at each church council meeting for six months. Then, with a unanimous uplifting of the Spirit, a collective aha! birthed new vision and life into the fragile congregation. As we named the potential ministry, each person was certain it was a direction from God, clearly the fruit from our practice of *lectio divina*. Unity and excitement were the marks of the Spirit's leading. The excitement could not be contained. The leadership team passionately spoke at the next Sunday worship and encouraged others to join in the ministry. The next week eighty-year-olds were on the floor or climbing ladders with paint or mop in hand. TheLifewell Free Store was prayed into existence.

The congregation transformed empty rooms into possibility; an ecumenical board was formed to govern the Free Store. The connectional United Methodist Church sent supportive presence to the store's opening. A television broadcast about the grand opening of an "unusual store" where no money changed hands brought the first throngs of people to theLifewell Free Store.

Enthusiasm and passion for ministry grew as community mission expanded. People once hesitant to pray aloud became advocates for prayer, and they continue to kneel in awe of God's mission and ministry explosion on the corner of Pierce and Putnam. Prayer and mission in this congregation have transformed life in the neighborhood and in the church. A gentle-spirited seventy-year-old woman sums up the miraculous power of praying the scripture for discernment and mission. Her words still ring in my heart: "Why hasn't any pastor ever before in all my years of going here taught us to pray like this?"

In previous chapters, we have looked at classic disciplines for Christian formation established in the early centuries of Christianity. The book of James also speaks of the important discussion about service to the world in the early church. In this chapter we turn more directly to applying faith to works and how we discern that relationship.

As early Christians sought to imitate Christ, many retreated into desert regions of Palestine, Syria, and Egypt. These women and men, called the desert mothers and fathers, shaped Christian practice in profound ways. Life in the desert eventually evolved into monastic communities. By the time Saint Benedict codified the rule of such community in the sixth century, it was clear that each day must be ordered around three fundamental principles—work, worship, and study of scripture. The term *lectio divina* refers to prayerful listening for divine inspiration from scripture. Added to this practice were two great "works": the "work of God," what we call worship (in Latin, *opus dei);* and the "work of the hands" *(opus manuum).* The everyday rhythm of Christian life was ordered around gathering for worship or the daily office of prayer, several hours for *lectio divina,* and the physical work essential for sustaining life. A fourth principle in *The Rule of St. Benedict* runs through the other three, the expectation of hospitality for one another in community and for any who seek rest, healing, or food.

Many voices today urge congregations to become "vital." This ancient model tells us what we need in order to do so: worship (*opus dei*), study prayerfully (*lectio divina*), and work together (*opus manuum*), in a spirit of generosity toward one another and our world (hospitality). These rules are all that we need for Christian churches to flourish. And the church will not be faithful or vital if we do not practice them in essential balance.

In the daily life of an early monastic community, monks gathered seven times a day for the *opus dei*—the recitation of the Psalms, scripture reading, and Holy Communion. They devoted themselves to *lectio divina* for up to four hours per day—devotional reading and meditation. For the remainder of the day they engaged in *opus manuum,* such as farming, cooking, building and building maintenance, care for guests, teaching children as schools were developed, or serving their neighbors in various ways. These monastic communities became integral to the functioning of their neighboring communities.

A modern-day Benedictine monastery in Germany, Abbey Koe-nigsmuenster, illustrates this interconnection of the *opus dei* in the monastery and the *opus manuum* of the community. Each autumn neighboring farmers bring bushels of apples from their orchards to be pressed at the abbey into cider. At that abbey, the daily afternoon service of the Eucharist is open to the broader community, and people flock in for Mass. There is a school for neighborhood children, a retreat center for summer youth camps as well as ongoing retreats for adults, and major programming open to all in concerns of spiritual life. Could our contemporary congregations in communities large and small be as vital to the life of all people within our parish area? Brenda Buckwell has described how First United Methodist Church in Zanesville, Ohio, became integral to its community. She reports that conversations between church members and visitors to the store have led First UMC to assist persons with an array of issues. The-Lifewell Free Store is an oasis of hospitality for the neighborhood.

Let's look at some more examples of people inviting the Spirit into their discernment for service (*opus manuum*). *Opus manuum* in the context of contemporary church issues encompasses two aspects— service in administrative tasks and service in community or world mission. The word *ministry* is embedded in the word *administration*. The tasks of *opus manuum* include both direct *ministries* and the duties of *administry*, the tasks that order our life together and facilitate outreach and mission. All too often, these various functions have been compartmentalized, losing their interrelatedness.

A MODEL FOR PERSONAL
AND CORPORATE DISCERNMENT

BRIAN WHITE LINKS individuals seeking a deeper personal spiritual life with their capacity to exercise leadership in the church. His diagram on the next page shows the significance of the intersection between personal devotional life and inspired discernment for ministry service. As a reader of this book, you are a Christian leader. This model can apply to all persons—lay and ordained—who want to offer leadership in mission and service.

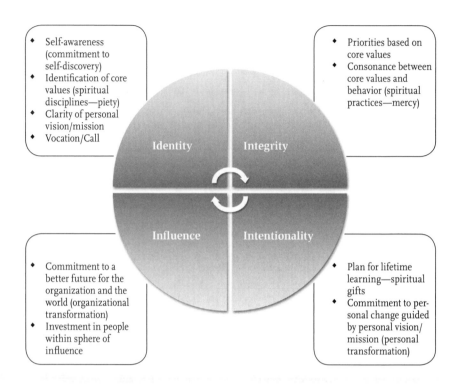

- Self-awareness (commitment to self-discovery)
- Identification of core values (spiritual disciplines—piety)
- Clarity of personal vision/mission
- Vocation/Call

- Priorities based on core values
- Consonance between core values and behavior (spiritual practices—mercy)

Identity   **Integrity**

Influence   **Intentionality**

- Commitment to a better future for the organization and the world (organizational transformation)
- Investment in people within sphere of influence

- Plan for lifetime learning—spiritual gifts
- Commitment to personal change guided by personal vision/mission (personal transformation)

Brian White developed this model while pastor of United Methodist Temple in Terre Haute, Indiana. He describes how spiritual leadership can be developed throughout congregational life:

> The beginning point for being an effective spiritual leader is to be a spiritual person. This is both an opportunity and a danger. A common foible for pastors is to feel that being the pastoral leader means being superspiritual. In their book *Leaders That Last*, authors Kinnaman and Ells state that "the pastor/leader must be spiritually minded, but he or she need not be the most spiritual person in the church."[2] This is a reminder to respect the spiritual journeys of those around us. Being honest about our spiritual shortcomings and leaning on the spiritual help of others can be a growth opportunity for all involved. W. Paul Jones, pastor, professor, priest, and spiritual director, says, "The first step in refashioning the local church around the dynamics of spiritual direction is for the pastor-priest to receive serious spiritual direction."[3]

There are at least two ways that spiritual growth can shape the life of a congregation. One way is through spiritual formation programs.

While that method helps people mature in faith, it has limitations. In the second approach to spiritual growth, spiritual practices are infused into every aspect of church life. In *Transforming Church Boards into Communities of Spiritual Leaders,* Charles M. Olsen suggests a method of administration that focuses on discernment within a spiritual/administrative context.

The separation between spiritual growth activities and the administrative functions of the church can create an unhealthy dichotomy, described by Charles Olsen as he fielded comments from people trying to implement his recommendations: "Paradoxically, two of the most frequent complaints were (1) 'It's run just like a business' and (2) 'It's not run enough like a business'! . . . One camp looked for efficiency models from business, while the other camp sought a whole different way of being a board that would draw from the culture of faith communities."[4] "Resistance to framing the work of a board as worship tends to come from the conviction that 'there is a place for everything and everything should be in its place.' Worship belongs to Sunday and sanctuary. Bible study belongs to Sunday school. Prayer belongs to worship."[5]

Olsen also asserts that "people are hungry for inspiration—in worship, in vocations, in family life. The church looks for inspirational leadership, usually from pastors. But why not from the board as well? Could not the council be inspired or 'in-spirited' and in turn provide inspiration for the whole church?"[6]

Because pastors are often poor at administration, laypeople feel compelled to apply principles that have worked in their secular vocations without integrating an understanding of biblical principles. The irony is that laypeople want the church to be different from business while wanting it to be more efficient.

A parishioner in a church I served resisted scheduling administrative council meetings on Sunday evening because she felt Sunday should be reserved solely for the sacred. The assumption behind her complaint was that doing administrative work was not sacred. Olsen observes:

> Just as the altar, the place of offering, is sacred and set apart, so the board room is holy ground. The board table is no less important than the communion table. Both are receptacles and distribution centers for sacred gifts.

When the gathering around a board table is intentionally prayerful and worshipful, it seems natural for all the aspects of a worship service, including the offering, to find their way in. But instead of passing the plate for money, the "stuff" of the meeting is lifted, released, and dedicated to God.[7]

Even a quick reading of the Acts of the Apostles demonstrates the prayerful way that the early church approached church administration. The complete integration of Spirit and order in the early church is a goal worthy of our aspirations.

PRAYER THAT LEADS TO MISSION

WHILE BRIAN WHITE promotes the link between administration and worship, many people also point to the necessity of prayer as inspiration for mission. We can only marvel at the movement of the Holy Spirit in the hearts and actions of individuals who find their sense of mission from prayer. And stories similar to the creation of theLifewell Free Store demonstrate that the size of a group or congregation does not matter. One inspired individual can lead others to mission; a small congregation can do the seemingly impossible with imagination and conviction.

Think again of the scene at Pentecost with "each person hearing in their own native language" (Acts 2:8, paraphrase). Again and again in Jesus' encounters, we note specificity. Particular individuals are addressed in their need and in their context. People are not asked to do everything but instead to be members of Christ, the Vine, as particular branches. Amazing power is unleashed when we become fully present to the particularity of calling in our own heart and in the immediate neighborhood of our congregations. Unique gifts flow within each of the following stories. Eugenia Gamble tells of discerning a mission to assist the homeless in Birmingham, Alabama. Gene Turner describes the passion that took him and a member of his two-point charge to Liberia. Cindy Serio recounts her call to be present with incarcerated women. Eugenia begins:

Old First Church was built in the nineteenth century by the steel barons, who, inspired by the rich veins of iron ore in Appalachia's southern foothills, determined to make a Pittsburgh of the South in the new city of Birmingham, Alabama. First Presbyterian Church was just that, the first church in the new model city. The church grew and prospered, taking pride to this day in being the church that sent the famed and beloved preacher Peter Marshall to seminary.

Beneath the prosperity, however, lay the soul-grinding reality of Jim Crow laws. There was more than one Birmingham, and that could not go on forever. With the growing civil rights movement and Dr. Martin Luther King Jr.'s efforts and subsequent jailing, things changed. When Dr. King wrote his famous *Letter from the Birmingham Jail*, addressed to, among others, the pastor of First Church, the Session voted to open the church to all of God's people. Half of God's people who were already there left immediately; and First Church, proud of its honorable stance, nevertheless entered into a decades-long period of numerical decline. That decline led also to a kind of institutional spiritual despair. Would the church be lost? Is it worth the struggle? Why do our children not share our faith? Does it really matter that we drive past dozens of other churches to make our way downtown to worship? Is there something more than a building and a heritage to preserve?

Regardless of the struggles, First Church remained a force for justice ministries in the city. After a fierce and uncharacteristic cold snap in the winter of 1983, in which two homeless neighbors froze on the streets, First Church opened its shelter for homeless women and children in the basement of the church. By the time I arrived as pastor in the mid-1990s, the saints at First Church knew we needed to do more. So, with a core of committed members and leaders and a church budget that was already $100,000 greater than pledges, First Church determined to acquire an old hotel a block from the church and turn it into a shelter for homeless women and children. This would require raising $2.5 million for the capital work alone. That is just what we did, and the center, First Light, has been in operation for twelve years now, the mortgage paid off in five years. First Church continues to be a thriving congregation with innovative ministries in many different areas.

Over the years, as I have told the First Church story, people have asked me how it happened. How did a small and struggling congregation have the courage and determination to take on such massive new ministries? Looking back, I credit two sources of the congregation's actions. First was our belief that we were doing the will of God. The second source was prayer. We entered into a nine-month School of Prayer. Each Wednesday evening at our fellowship supper, 70 percent of our worshiping congregation gathered to learn about and practice prayer. Each week I taught for thirty minutes on a different aspect of the life of prayer. With a guide I prepared ahead of time, participants spent the last thirty minutes in small groups around tables praying together according to the pattern we had just explored. Drawing on the rich traditions of Christian spiritual practice, each week's session addressed a contemporary need. For example: How do I pray when I feel stressed? How do I pray for forgiveness? How do I listen to God? We learned how to enter into silence together, how to speak to God together, how to pray our grief, our talents, and our fears. We experienced writing in a journal and dancing to a psalm. We learned the art of lament and the healing prayer of laughter. We became a praying whole.

On the first evening, one of the older members of the church came up to me as I was about to begin. She was angry and threatening to go home after the supper. "I'm mad as a hornet, Eugenia," she said. "I have been a Christian all my life. All of that time I have been told to pray about this or that and nobody has ever taught me how. I don't want to learn *about* prayer. I want to learn to pray." She stayed, as did the rest of the flock. Nine months later we were building a $2.5 million shelter.

Gene Turner, a United Methodist pastor serving a two-point charge in Illinois, describes inviting the Spirit into a discernment about mission:

I had felt God calling me to go on a mission trip, so I asked the Administrative Councils of the congregations I served to pray with me and for me in the discernment of where I was to go in March of 2008. About three months later I attended a district clergy meeting where a Liberian pastor spoke. This pastor described watching his father being killed by a man during the civil conflict in Liberia. After the conflict, which lasted from 1990 to 2003, was over, this man became a Christian. He worshiped in the Liberian pastor's church. One Communion Sunday, the pastor had to decide if he would offer Holy Communion to the man who murdered his father. As I listened to the story, God spoke to me: "Go to Liberia; they have something you need!"

At the next Administrative Council meetings, I shared with the respective boards what I had experienced. In one session, a man from whom

I least expected a response stood up and said, "If our pastor says he needs to go, I don't care if we have to borrow every cent, we are sending him!" When the council meeting was over, a soft-spoken woman named Sharon waited until everyone was gone and then approached me. "Can I help you with this trip?" she asked. I responded by saying, "I will not presume to know what you mean by that question. Please tell me more." She said, "Can I go with you? I have wanted to go on a mission trip for a long time, but I don't want to go alone." Thus began a four-month period of preparation to travel over seven thousand miles from home.

Our conference does not send groups of less than ten people for economic reasons. When the time came for the final decision on the Liberia mission, only seven people were committed. The missions coordinator said, "I cannot cancel this trip. This group is unique, and they must experience Liberia."

Sharon and I experienced Liberia, and what an impact it made on both of us. We left Liberia pledged to make a difference in any way we could in the lives of the people we had met. We had experienced radical hospitality[8] and would never spiritually be the same again. On the flight home from Liberia, Sharon and I exchanged thoughts and ideas. For her, observing people using buckets to draw water out of a shallow pool located far from their homes had motivated her to give money for digging a well. A well would give these people safe, clean, easily accessible water. We both were determined to enable some of the children we met to attend school.

Upon our return, the mission team shared pictures and stories of the people and children we had met with the two congregations that I served (Stronghurst and Carman churches of the Illinois Great Rivers Conference). We also had the privilege of sharing our stories in numerous other churches, and we dedicated any stipends or funds raised from speaking to scholarships for the Liberian children.

As a result of the hands-on mission, Sharon grew spiritually by taking a more active role in leadership, starting a young women's fellowship group and spearheading fund-raisers for local food pantries and scholarships for Liberian children. I grew spiritually by learning to trust God's leading, and by inviting and leading those two congregations to pray, give, and engage in Jesus' call to discipleship.

Both Sharon and I have been sustained by the prayers of others during times of difficulty and frustration, as well as by responses from the children who have had the opportunity to go to school in Liberia. We continue to see and feel God's hand at work in the lives of the Liberian people as well as in our own sense of trust and faith in God to provide what we need.

Discerning mission can begin in the prayer of a single individual. Cindy Serio relates her calling to offer spiritual direction in a women's prison:

As I contemplate the ministry of holy listening in the context of women impacted by incarceration, I envision the image of "witness." As I listen, I bear witness to their deep pain. Often, the pain strikes such a resonant chord within me I fear I cannot bear it. And yet, as each sacred story unfolds, God moves in with unconditional love and healing grace.

"Listen, Listen, Love, Love" is the guiding principle of Kairos Prison Ministry International, through which I first experienced the sharing of sacred stories. When one hears the call to holy listening with persons impacted by incarceration, it helps to spend time in a well-established restorative justice ministry early in the discernment process to clarify the call and explore the question: *Can I be a witness to the pain of incarcerated persons without becoming a captive myself, either to my own pain or to my own avoidance of pain?*

One morning as I was meditating on Luke 4:18, these words shimmered off the page straight into my heart: "proclaim release to the captives." Suddenly I knew God was sending me to the women at a local prison. After a long conversation with the chaplain, he asked me why I was there and I was honest: "I don't know. I only know that God wants me to be here." He smiled a knowing smile and said, "Follow me."

As I followed the chaplain, we traveled a long and winding path to the area set apart for women residents. Female security guards watched over everyone from an elevated room with a view into three pods. Each pod held about thirty women and was completely self-contained—large rooms with individual bunks, toilets, showers, and sinks in full view, one monitor for visitation behind a curtain, and four metal lunch tables by the entrance of the pod. For a while I was embarrassed by the lack of dignity I perceived, but that faded as the pods became familiar to me.

We approached the first pod, and I turned to the chaplain. "What am I supposed to do now?" He said, "Listen. Just listen. The ladies will let you know what they need." He exited rather abruptly, which left me feeling a little lost. (I often felt lost in the ensuing months, but when that happened, I would take a deep breath and remember to just listen.) Over time my trust in God deepened. After the chaplain left me alone, I sat at one of the metal tables. Women came and shared their sacred stories, which ranged from terrifically terrifying to merely mundane. An hour passed, and the ladies sent me to the next pod. This "sit, listen, move" pattern would become my Monday-afternoon rhythm over the next two years as I grew in my capacity to hold the healing space through holy listening.

Listen. Just Listen. Every week held a new surprise. Some weeks I didn't know anyone who came to the table. Some weeks, I knew everyone. Some weeks were chaotic; some, quiet. Some weeks there were many interruptions; some, none. One of the ladies told me, "You are the only one who gives us hugs." Another one said, "After you leave, there is a peace in this place." I guess there were as many reasons as there were women who came to sit with me. I was humbled.

Listen. Just Listen. Some weeks a small need would emerge in their stories that I could meet. The King James Bible, so often donated but so hard to read! I created a resource to bring to the table. It was one page with a scripture passage (*New Living Translation*), reflection questions, and a prayer. One of the ladies told me, "Some of the women are too scared to come and sit with you, so I take the sheet back and we study and pray together." I was humbled.

Listen. Just Listen. Some weeks a small need would emerge in their stories that I couldn't meet on my own. "Panties, you have no panties!" The church responded anonymously with lots and lots of panties. Miraculously it seemed the ladies had panties, and I experienced the joy of seeing, in the words of Mother Teresa, these "small things [given] with great love."[9] I was humbled.

Listen. Just Listen. The sacred story will unfold. Can I get a witness?

A RETREAT FOR CONGREGATIONAL DISCERNMENT

BRIAN WHITE'S STORY challenges us to integrate spiritual discernment into all kinds of decision processes. But how shall we do so? Brenda Buckwell offers one effective method: spending time each month with a group *lectio divina* process, inviting God's guidance for direction in ministry. Nancy LeValley describes teaching spiritual formation practices within the context of the board meeting in chapter 1. Eugenia Gamble taught methods of prayer to 70 percent of a whole congregation; subsequently, congregational mission arose in a profound way. The accounts from Cindy Serio and Gene Turner show what can happen when individuals answer the call to mission and engage others in that vision.

How can congregational leaders—lay and clergy—encourage prayerful discernment in all areas of church life? A model I have used with many congregations for periodically discerning mission and ministry is a planning retreat based on John 15:1-11, in which Jesus calls himself "the true vine." The text provides a window into the communal nature of life in Christ. If we imagine the "branches" as the particular ministries of any congregation, we readily see their interconnectedness; they all spring from Christ, the Vine. The description of the sprouting, growing, pruning, and decaying of all natural plants enables us to see our ministries as subject to the same cycles of growth and diminishment.

To design your own retreat for discernment of ministry and mission, begin by deciding the scope of the work. This process can be used effectively for a single work area or for an overview of all ministry areas.[10] Persons for each designated area would be present. A three-hour time block can encompass the retreat, but if it's possible to work at a more leisurely pace, plan a four- to six-hour retreat, with time for lunch fellowship. Adapt the following retreat outline to your setting. Inviting the Spirit into discernment in this way can initiate a journey of discovery and fruitfulness.

A RETREAT OUTLINE

Preparation. Arrange tables to seat six to eight people each, with some magazines or pictures cut from magazines on the tables, as well as colored pens, scissors, and glue sticks. Prepare large pieces of newsprint, one for each table. Draw part of a branch of a vine on each piece of newsprint ahead of time. Make a central piece that depicts the main vine, including its roots. I intentionally make this a rather crude production so that people do not worry about artistic ability. Something like this:

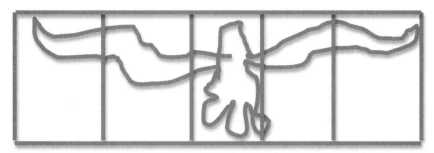

Keep the central piece out for use later or post it on a wall large enough to accommodate the other pieces alongside it later, as people report on their findings.

Plan to give people time to refresh themselves regarding issues of concern, ask questions of one another, and build a shared understanding of what is actually happening in ministry areas or around issues to be discussed during the retreat. You may discover that people are not well informed. This exercise itself can be very helpful for the spirit of your congregation. Depending upon the knowledge base of participants regarding the particular ministry areas you plan to explore, prepare a worksheet to gather current perceptions about them. List the ministry areas you intend to examine, with space for people to write in their observations, comments, or concerns. All work areas could be listed, such as Children's Sunday School, Youth Program, Adult Education, Worship, Building and Grounds, Mission, Hospitality, Evangelism, and so on. Or if you intend a more focused planning retreat—for example, working only in the education area—gather input on that single area. These worksheets will be used in the "Gathering information" portion of the retreat.

Also prepare worksheets for the exercise "Exploring the themes in John 15." See questions to include below in that section.

Getting started. In advance, decide whether to seat people in work area groups or "mix it up" by seating people from different ministry areas together. Guide people to tables accordingly when they arrive.

• Open with prayer and a song. Ask people to find a picture among the options on the table that describes something they really like about your church. Spend a few minutes allowing people to browse through the magazines, tearing out a picture that speaks to them.

• Ask people to introduce themselves to their tablemates using the picture selected. Tell everyone to keep their picture handy (these will likely turn up on their piece of newsprint a bit later).

• Read John 15:1-11 aloud together. Then pause for silence, inviting people to listen for a particular word or phrase that inspires them in this reading. After a minute or so of silence, ask each person to share the word or phrase with others at the table, particularly as it may relate to the task you have set for the day.

Gathering information. Use the worksheets you prepared to gather current understandings about the various issues or work areas you are addressing at the retreat. Ask people to fill these out for themselves, before speaking together. Then, give each person a specified amount of time to share themes of importance to them that emerge from this exercise, as well as to get any information corrected by others.

Take a break!

Exploring the themes in John 15. Prepare a worksheet for each individual, with space for responding to the questions below. State a theme for reflection as the heading for the worksheet, based on your retreat focus.

1. What is growing well and producing good fruit?
2. What is growing well but could use pruning (attention) to be more fruitful?
3. What is deadwood? That is, what is no longer life-giving? Perhaps you continue a ministry out of habit or loyalty to what worked in times past. Think also of attitudes that are hindering you.
4. What is ready to sprout?

The leader or another individual reads John 15:1-11 again to the group. Add some commentary about the aspects of growth of a vine, the need for pruning, the sense that God is the gardener, and the obvious sense that all plants grow for a while, then some branches wither and need to be cut off, and others need to be pruned like the grapevine. The grapevine will always put out more blooms than can be sustained to grow into grapes; hence, it must be pruned to be fruitful. Suggest the group recall various ministries of the church that grew for a time but have faded in significance. Are there some now that might be allowed to die out altogether, in order to make room for new growth?

Invite participants into some group thinking about their roots as a congregation. Write responses around the roots drawn on the illustration of your central vine as they are mentioned.

Now move to individual reflection. Hand out the prepared worksheets with theme and reflection questions. Allow time for people to write their responses to the questions.

Take a break!

When people return to their table groups, invite them to share their comments one question at a time. Encourage them to begin drawing and labeling their ideas on the vine illustration. They can glue their pictures onto their piece of the vine. You don't need to do much at this point in terms of guidance. People seem to get right to work. Someone will emerge as the scribe/artist. Others will cut out more pictures. Be prepared for a burst of creative energy as people engage their creative thinking with images and colors. Monitor your time, being sure that each group gets to all of the questions.

Also be sure each group notes the deadwood, perhaps drawing some dead branches or even drawing a bonfire of them.

Remind everyone to keep track of what is ready to sprout.

Reporting. Put up each part of the vine as groups give verbal reports. After each group has reported, come to a consensus about what ministries should be noted as ready to sprout. You can draw and label these as sprouts at the top of the central section of the vine. When this is done, give every person two sticky dots; ask them to place these on the two sprouts most important for them.

Stress that all of their work in this retreat provides information that the church administrative body will receive for conversation and implementation. Frequently groups find the resulting vine image so useful they want to display it prominently in their church building, along with a detailed written report on their findings.

Closing. Close the table groups by reading the scripture again, listening now for the invitation to the congregation. Ask someone at each table to note the invitations named at their table for future reference. Ask people to pray for the invitation heard by the person to their right and for their congregation. If time does not permit praying aloud around the circle, everyone may pray silently at the same time. The leader or a volunteer may close the retreat with prayer and benediction.

◆ ◆ ◆

This retreat model works well for congregations of varying sizes and situations, as well as for not-for-profit boards. I'm always amazed at the level of buzz created when the table groups start getting into their own conversation, drawing on the newsprint, cutting out and pasting pictures. Universally, groups are able to name the "deadwood" that holds them back.

One congregation had been stuck on an issue related to their building for twenty years. Under "deadwood" they named their own stuckness in this process. And they found a way to laugh together at themselves to get over what had impeded them for so long. A task force was charged with highlighting their own history through skits presented in worship and cartoonlike depictions in the church newsletter.

Another congregation decided after a day retreat using this format that they could no longer put off air-conditioning their sanctuary. A small family rural church near a major metropolitan area decided to build a fellowship hall onto their modest country church building. The fellowship hall has enabled them to accommodate visitors and shift from being a family church to being a church in service to their community.

> You have heard that it was said, "You shall love your neighbor and hate your enemy." But I say to you, Love your enemies and pray for those who persecute you, so that you may be children of your Father in heaven; for he makes his sun rise on the evil

and on the good, and sends rain on the righteous and on the unrighteous. For if you love those who love you, what reward do you have? Do not even the tax collectors do the same? And if you greet only your brothers and sisters, what more are you doing than others? Do not even the Gentiles do the same? Be perfect, therefore, as your heavenly Father is perfect.—Matthew 5:43-48

To follow Jesus is to be continuously pushing our own boundaries in loving our neighbor. This task becomes joy when it is coupled with continuously pushing our boundaries to loving God. In too many cases our lives of mission are too separate from the life of prayer. By inviting the Spirit into mission discernment, we move toward balancing the guiding principles of healthy church life:

- practicing our *opus mannum*, our life of service, in tandem with our *opus dei*, our life of worship, prayer, and praise
- practicing *hospitality* as an outgrowth of faith deepened by praying the scriptures, *lectio divina*

Perhaps like the sincere folks in Zanesville, Ohio, we have narrowed our sense of mission so much that we've forgotten to look outside our walls and invite our community to participate with us in new life. Perhaps we are ready for God to burst our self-imposed barriers, as they were inspired to do. Perhaps it's time to more faithfully practice loving God with all of our heart and soul and mind and strength *and* our neighbor as ourselves (Matt. 22:37-39; Mark 12:30-31; Luke 10:27).

CHAPTER FOUR

Inviting the Spirit into
AGE-LEVEL MINISTRIES

*The angel said to her, "The Holy Spirit will come
upon you; . . .
therefore the child to be born will be holy;
he will be called Son of God.
And now, your relative Elizabeth in her old age has
also conceived a son;
and this is the sixth month for her who was said to
be barren.
For nothing will be impossible with God."*
—Luke 1:35-37

THE HOLY SPIRIT is working within us whether we are young, old, or somewhere in between. Like Mary and her cousin Elizabeth in the birth narrative of Jesus, God has something in store for us both in youth and in age. In this chapter we will hear from people at work in spiritual formation ministries with young and elder adults. Both brim with the work of the Holy Spirit dwelling among us. We are invited to set aside assumptions regarding ministry with these two groups and observe how spiritual formation practices allow God to speak across the generations.

YOUNG ADULT MINISTRIES

WE FREQUENTLY HEAR of the spiritual challenges faced by youth and young adults, particularly that they are not open to the life of the Spirit. Silence, prayer, creative expression, and life reflection undermine this false assertion and invite pastors, parents, and teachers to take faith issues among youth and young adults seriously and provide opportunities for experiential awakening and sharing.

Jeff Druery and Marybeth Leis Druery describe their innovative use of reflection circles and "tech-free spaces" at McMaster University in campus ministry through Student Open Circles, a charity based in Hamilton, Ontario:

Why are so many young adults not participating in traditional faith communities? And where do these "spiritual but not religious" types find sustenance and supportive community?

Student Open Circles campus ministry emerged in 2001 at McMaster University.[1] At the time, approximately fifteen Christian groups were active on campus in addition to other major faith groups, but no safe space existed where students who did not identify with a particular religious faith could explore their spirituality.

We began very small, by engaging in conversation with a few students and their friends and listening to their perspectives and questions. We noticed that young people are not looking for more information about God or faith. They are looking for communities they can be a part of that will support them in their formation. They are longing for experiential approaches to spirituality to help them reflect and find meaning in their lives. And they are looking to discover and live from their authentic values and true self. We've followed the students' lead and supported them in discovering the practices and vocabulary that resonated with them.

Ten years later, Student Open Circles provides forums for group reflection, creative and spiritual practices, and community service for students from a variety of faith and nonreligious backgrounds. We offer weekly groups for discussion and reflection, events, retreats, and individual spiritual direction. We also coordinate a network of weekly volunteer groups where over three hundred students serve in children's tutoring programs, working with adults living with disabilities, with recent immigrants, at homeless shelters, and in other programs that address the needs of our local community. In all our activities we maintain a strong emphasis on leadership development, so that the students take ownership of their involvement in the community. We provide resources, coaching, skills training, and ask evocative questions that encourage individual and group reflection.

We have discovered three experiential gateways to spiritual and personal transformation in particular that are important for many young adults: creativity, reflection, and service.

Creative practices like art and music can take students beyond the level of mere intellect in order to touch upon something deeper. Our monthly open-mike coffeehouse provides a relaxed atmosphere where people can express themselves through music, poetry, art, and story. There is no program or script to follow. It is like a potluck meal where people gather to experience community and be spiritually nourished. In our weekly Creativity Circle, students engage in visual art and other creative expressions in a variety of media and reflect upon what they have created, allowing creativity to cultivate spiritual formation and growth.

For many young adults, attending an hour-long reflection group would be a huge leap, which is why we offer a weekly "Tech-Free Zone" where students can drop in and engage in a variety of alternative activities such as painting, discussion, playing games, quiet reading, and study. It might not look like a typical spiritual retreat, but it is a rest from the pressures and distractions of student life. In addition to breaking the habit of checking their cell phones every ten minutes, students tell us they are discovering a new sense of community with peers as they talk about their lives, families, and things more important than YouTube. In one instance a student was moved to tears after just fifteen seconds of silence; she had never before experienced this much distraction-free space.

Many young adults are keenly aware of the global problems we are facing and want to be involved in creating a better world. In our weekly volunteer groups, we empower students to make a positive difference in our local community and encourage them to reflect upon their service. In each volunteer group, a student facilitator leads a weekly reflection activity where volunteers explore the ways their service connects to their own life path and broader issues of social justice. In this way volunteering can become an important practice for spiritual formation.

Jennie Edwards Bertrand writes of the 24/7 prayer room movement[2] and its influence on her work in campus ministry at Illinois State University:

In September 1999 in a village in southern England, Pete Greig and his college friends decided that if the Moravians could pull off a one-hundred-year prayer vigil, they could sustain three months of unbroken prayer. It seemed like a great way to induct the year 2000.[3] What this group did not know was how news of their small prayer room would spread to college students and young adults all over the world by e-mail. Prayer rooms began to pop up all over the world, run mostly by young adults.

While the phrase "I am not religious, I am spiritual" was quite popular as we were preparing for our first 24/7 prayer room, I don't think many of the students were consciously concerned about their spiritual lives either. Looking back, I think the main reason that first group of thirty students was willing to try a prayer room was because it sounded crazy and undoable. They were competitive and wanted to be able to say, "We kept a human in that room for one hundred and sixty-eight hours. . . . Oh yeah, and they were praying."

If Richard Foster had known about the 24/7 prayer movement that was underway while he was writing *Streams of Living Water*, it could have been included in his Contemplative Stream. "We all hunger for a prayer-filled life, for a richer, fuller practice of the presence of God," writes Foster.[4] The only corrective I add to this is that a generation raised in a postmodern, post-Christian world doesn't know it hungers for a prayer-filled life. One of my favorite characteristics of the 24/7 prayer movement is that the participants are not limited to those who would self-select to attend a prayer retreat, or join a prayer group.

A student leader and I collected paints and canvases, and covered the floor with cardboard and the walls with newsprint. We bought a CD player, some good meditative CDs, and a few worship CDs. We labeled the space outside the small converted office the Welcome Wall; plenty of coffee and water was provided. We labeled one wall a Wailing Wall; another wall the Worship Wall; and on a third wall we hung a map and named it the World Wall. We included a stack of Bibles, two journals, and hooks on the wall for hanging painted canvases. We went to the Catholic supply store, bought twelve seven-day candles, and ritually lit each one. For one week, hour-by-hour, students experienced the presence of God in the solitude of this room. One person would write a psalm on the Worship Wall, and others would follow suit. Names of loved ones in need of healing and R.I.P.s began to fill the Wailing Wall. Confessions and expressions of pain followed. Articulate and painfully honest conversations with God began to fill the pages of the journals. Beautiful artistic expressions of love, forgiveness, and healing covered the canvases. People highlighted countries on the map and asked for prayer, justice, and the end of poverty and war. By the end of the week, the floor and every wall was filled with an outpouring of deep cries from the soul. Right in the middle of day-to-day life, an entire (albeit small) ministry learned how to pray and experienced the power of God's presence.

We are preparing for our sixth room at Illinois State, and it is a small miracle each time an eighteen- to twenty-two-year-old makes the decision to engage with our (or any) Christian faith community.

Melanie Baffes takes a different approach with high school girls in a nine-month spiritual companioning group:

The focus of the spiritual companioning group was to give high school girls a chance to explore who they are in relation to God by sharing faith stories with peers and finding meaning in their own spiritual narratives. Teaching a high school youth ministry group, I noticed how often the girls were quiet and participating halfheartedly. My sense was that this was not only because the boys tended to dominate but also because the activities weren't doing much for the girls. I had for some time been concerned about the challenges young women face—pressures to conform are exaggerated for girls who, by the time they reach high school, have received so many damaging messages about what it means to be a woman. They listen to the voices of others over their own and struggle to know who they are and how to fit in. I knew they were trying to figure out what they believed compared to what their religion told them to believe. I wanted to offer a safe space where they could explore spiritual questions.

The small group of eight to ten girls met on Friday nights for one school year, except for breaks or weekends of special school events. I would open each session with a brief prayer or ask one of the girls to do so, sending the message that whatever we discussed was in the context of faith. Usually, each girl would "check in," and we would settle on one topic or one girl's story. My role was to keep everyone focused on the question of God's presence (or absence) in their stories.

Facilitating this group solidified my desire to help women of all ages find meaning in their faith journeys—particularly those who do not have a space for this kind of exploration within the church. It also affirmed that telling stories gives shape and meaning to the faith journeys of women. Working with this group allowed me to discern my own strengths and to recognize the gift of being with others as they seek God's presence in their lives.[5]

We discussed the role of visual symbols in sensory-rich worship in chapter 2. Steve Braudt, artist and youth minister, describes the power of visual art to enliven the walls of the children's and youth areas at First United Methodist Church in Cedar Falls, Iowa. These projects involved the talents of children and youth:

Art as a spiritual discipline reflects a journey of spiritual discovery. It speaks of memories, dreams, and visions of what God is calling us to do. As an artist I have set out to create work and spaces that are open and engaging, so that all who view my art are invited to experience the Holy Spirit. "When we engage in the arts, we dip into our souls to discover deep pools of wonder, breath-taking gifts of beauty, and quiet revelation."[6] This has been my dream and vision since 1995 when I received my call from God. Since that day, I strive to live as colorful a life as I can. I desire to live a life of love, belief, prayer, and faith. I dip into my soul and share the gifts of wonder and beauty that God has shared with me. The church needs an infusion of creativity.

On the third floor of First United Methodist Church in Cedar Falls, Iowa, is a space now filled with the vision and passion of a group of dreamers willing to open themselves to the creative inspiration of the Holy Spirit. The words *Live, Love, Believe, Pray, Faith* explode from the wall, propelling individuals toward either a corporate faith journey or a more personal spiritual path.

The first room, the Harvest Café, offers nurture for the whole person, restoring the traveler's body and soul. Food is served with ample doses of scripture and Bible study. It is not uncommon to smell a home-cooked meal while hearing scripture read. The windows, transformed into a stained-glass sunrise, flood the room with holy light. A mural of a cornfield in the midst of a storm bears the words "The harvest is great . . . but the workers are few" (see Luke 10:2).

The game room is energized by a mural of the life of Christ. It reminds us of the struggle, victory, and promise yet to come. The mural, though designed by me, was a community project intended to engage the artistic expressions of persons ages six to sixty and represents the ongoing ministry of the church. The youth contributed their own ideas, dreams, and visions that were added to the story of Christ. "Engaging the arts in community is a wonderful support for an ongoing commitment to artistry and integration."[7]

Leaving this last room, we see four more walls covered in bright graffiti and bearing the words *Jesus, Way, Truth, Life*. Unlike the words that drew us into this space of color, experience, and renewal, these words lead us out into the world. We emerge buoyed by the knowledge that through Jesus, all things are possible.

The Creator did not give us the gifts of spirituality, love, compassion, vision, and wonder that we might live colorless spiritual lives. We are striving to recapture the tradition of witnessing to the power of the Holy Spirit in our lives and the transformational changes that have occurred by the grace of God. Laity—youth especially—are trained to pray, lead worship, and assist in serving the sacraments. We sing, pray, witness, teach the good news, and share Communion. Our dream is that all those present will experience Jesus in their midst.

SPIRITUAL FORMATION IN ELDER YEARS

JANNA BORN LARSEN is chaplain at a for-profit retirement center in the Chicago suburbs. The residents come from diverse faith backgrounds, and Janna has found creative ways to work with this variety of faith traditions:

It is difficult to describe my ministry in Sedgebrook, a continuing care retirement community, as "spiritual guidance," but indeed, at times I do engage in spiritual guidance. As pastoral ministries manager and chaplain, though I more often see my role as a community spiritual "enlovener"—one who ministers in order to love and enliven others to more fully embrace their own spiritual paths and experience how their spirituality can gift the community and beyond. Even with an average age of eighty-four, there is still plenty of bloom left on these roses, blooms of spiritual growth, gratitude, and celebration. The spiritual formation and exploration of our Interfaith Council is a case in point.

Sedgebrook is currently home to approximately 550 people in independent living (apartments) and forty people in assisted living or skilled nursing. Religious affiliations are about a quarter each from Protestant, Jewish, and Catholic traditions. The remaining quarter comprise people who (1) claim no religious affiliation; (2) whose religion is rare in the community; or (3) who are on a spiritual path that has no formal name. Thus, spiritual leadership and care take place within both an interreligious and an interspiritual community. Our weekly interfaith worship service encourages and sustains respect between people of various religions or spiritualities. Any and all are welcome, whether or not they practice a faith tradition or believe in God. This service and other interfaith/interspiritual activities provide a safe space where we can live into our motto to "honor our own tradition, honor the traditions of others, and honor who we are together." Leaders of the Jewish, Catholic, and Protestant councils demonstrate respect for each other and are invited to represent their faith communities in the work of a thirteen-member Interfaith Council.

The Interfaith Council members demonstrate interspiritual goodwill and an appreciation for the richness of ambiguity, creativity, imagination, and many spiritual points of view. The Interfaith Council started as a planning group in 2006 and has evolved. The council meets monthly and is cochaired by the pastoral ministries manager and a resident council member. Leadership is shared. All members of the Interfaith Council work together to accomplish a variety of tasks: creation of a vision and mission statement for the council, planning and sponsoring events and activities, and taking the pulse of the whole community. This discernment process is critical in a community with many different perspectives and nuances at play. They serve as ambassadors of community peace and goodwill.

Susan Amick, a chaplain for Sanctuary at Bellbrook in Rochester Hills, Michigan, offers a framework for spiritual formation for seniors in late age. It is based on the three plagues of aging described by Dr. William Thomas—loneliness, boredom, and helplessness:[8]

Practice of the spiritual disciplines can create a context for wholeness and spiritual vitality during late age. The model below shows the framework for a spiritual formation program:

Relationship vs. Loneliness. "For I am convinced that neither death, nor life, nor angels, nor rulers, nor things present, nor things to come, nor powers, nor height, nor depth, nor anything else in all creation, will be able to separate us from the love of God in Christ Jesus our Lord" (Rom. 8:38-39).

Spiritual Formation Connections in Late Age

Relationship   Loneliness
With God, Self, and Other . . .

                        | Alleviates |

Regeneration   Boredom
Learning and Growth . . . | OR |

Rationale | Moderates |
Purpose for Being . . .   Helplessness

Rest
Holy and Blessed Abiding ~ The Fruit of Practice

Aging can bring both physical and emotional isolation as one grieves a variety of losses. Sometimes elders feel alone and disconnected from God's abiding presence. The spiritual disciplines allow elders to grow near to God, to one another, and to themselves.

As people experience "the diminishments of our physical or mental capacities, we need companions for prayer and for support in prayer even when our own capacities for prayer may be waning."[9] Companions for the journey are essential in creating spiritual practices that are relationally significant, lasting, and supportive during this phase of life marked by both growth and surrender. There is still potential in age—potential best realized and affirmed in community.

Rationale/Purpose vs. Helplessness. Active, able elders need to have a sense of purpose. Elders with physical and cognitive limitations also need a reason for living and loving. People in their later years often ask the question *What use am I?* In God we have a purpose. Christians are called to "love the Lord your God with all your heart, and with all your soul, and with all your strength, and with all your mind; and your neighbor as yourself" (Luke 10:27). This call never ceases; it represents a lifetime of living in God. For too long, aging has been characterized solely as decrepitude and dependence leading to death. Eugene Bianchi comments that "a primary task for older people is to divest themselves of negative stereotypes of what it means to be old."[10] Gene Cohen talks about helping people "in the second half of life awaken the partnered powers of age and creativity to find a new sense of possibility. . . . Creativity is a catalyst for change of the best kind, with benefits that are immediate, long-lasting, and within the reach of every person."[11] Deep faith is formed through life experience and the long view of God's eternal sense of purpose.

Regeneration vs. Boredom. We are called to learn and grow in faith across a lifetime. For Methodists, this is an essential part of our faith tradition: "Not only did Wesley view growth in the Christian life as a continual possibility, it was his normative expectation."[12] "Life review for the elderly is not sufficient; they must also engage in a 'life preview.' This involves the fashioning of images of the future for themselves, their families, and society in general."[13] This is legacy building and gives meaning to both the waning generation and the generations that follow.

Rest: Holy and Blessed Abiding

Perfect submission, all is at rest;
I in my Savior am happy and blest,
watching and waiting, looking above,
filled with his goodness, lost in his love.
This is my story, this is my song,
Praising my savior all the day long;
this is my story, this is my song,
praising my savior all the day long.[14]

It is a blessing when the assurance of God's presence is real and true in both heart and mind. What creates this opportunity to know God's presence so confidently? I have sung this hymn at many bedsides; in part for the dying, in part for their family, and in part for me. I have met many people who have reached a place in life where they are assured of God's presence. Many elders long for a sense of peace, contentment, and assurance. Brian McLaren describes the final fruit of a life of prayer:

And now imagine the person who loves God and who therefore loves spiritual practices, but who also loves—can I say it this way?—*not* practicing them. Being in silence and at *rest* with God using no words at all—this is not the passive silence of emptiness, complacency, or negation, but rather the living silence that is pregnant with infinite possibilities.[15]

Spiritual disciplines can be the bridge between lonely despair and faithful hope as elders struggle to know God's joy and purpose. Faith is joyfully fueled by spiritual practices that enable a creative perspective toward growth throughout late age. Each day I witness spiritual disciplines in action: Sandra faithfully gathers with a small group of charismatic Catholics each week to explore new spiritual practices; Elizabeth prays the Rosary with her small community six days each week; Arthur walks outside daily, reading scripture passages tucked away in his pocket when he needs a rest. These ordinary people demonstrate strong faith and unheralded practices that create and sustain connections to God and God's creation.

HEALTH AND WELLNESS MINISTRY

A PARISH NURSE at Faith United Presbyterian Church in Farmers Branch, Texas, Kay McLellan blends health concerns and spirituality in her work with persons sixty-five and older in her health and wellness ministry and helps us think about health and wellness components in terms of spiritual formation:

We learn from the Bible that much of Jesus' ministry was directed toward the sick. He healed in miraculous ways. He touched the inner part of people and restored wholeness and the joy of a new beginning in this life on earth. He also instructed the disciples to heal. Two nurses at our church wanted to be such disciples, so we created a Ministry of Health and Wellness. This ministry began with the goal of nurturing those in the congregation who were struggling with health problems. It is widely known that when you are sick, you are sick all over—body, mind, and spirit. Your life is put on hold while your thoughts, feelings, and energy are directed toward getting well. Restoring balance in your life is essential for work, family, and caring for yourself. When faced with puzzling health problems, you lose your perspective on life. Christians turn to God for redemption from the bodily misery, anxiety, and loss of self that come with illness. We decided to make ourselves available to help others find solutions to health problems and to support their efforts to find God in their illness.

The two parish nurses in our congregation assist individuals to learn about their disease, to find community resources, to talk with their physicians, and to evaluate information from various sources. We guide them as they adjust to a different way of living while waiting for God's healing presence. We listen, teach, counsel, and refer them, as necessary, to health providers in the community. For the members of our church it is like having an educated professional as a personal friend. The parish nurse is dedicated to a person's well-being in body, mind and spirit; spends time with individuals as a friend; and protects privacy by keeping information confidential.

Much of the interaction between parish nurses and patients in our church takes place in a private space provided for the health ministry. The room is equipped with a sphygmomanometer, scales, thermometer, and first-aid supplies. We have a computer to do Internet searches and a DVD player to access health information provided in that form. There is also a library of books and other materials and current newsletters on various topics, such as disease symptoms, medications, anatomy and physiology, first aid, diet, exercise, relationships, and spirituality, to aid the patient in becoming more skilled in researching self-care.

The nurses are members of the church and attend worship and other groups that are part of the church's ministry. This affords members casual opportunities to observe the nurse as a role model for health and to talk about health issues. To protect trust, we avoid sharing information about the health problems of others with the congregation.

To maintain competence and knowledge of current medical and nursing practices, we are affiliated with a faith community nurse program at Texas Health Presbyterian Hospital in Dallas. The program organizes conferences and provides opportunities to earn CEUs to maintain licensure.

Working with older parishioners has helped me in my own struggles with aging and mortality, and has provided me the comfort of knowing I am not alone. I thank God daily for my education and the opportunity to share it with others in ministry.

Over a decade ago, I learned about a unique congregational focus at First United Methodist Church in Omaha, Nebraska. Their Health, Spiritual Formation, and Care Ministries group oversees prayer ministries, the church's Stephen Ministry, health screenings, and many other aspects of congregational care and spiritual formation.[16] This comprehensive program models Christ's attention to physical and emotional well-being and provides an example of what Christian healing means.

In this chapter we have focused on youth, young adults, and elder adults. These age-groups are quite open to the ancient/modern practices of prayer and reflection. The insights from campus ministries, as well as the interfaith ministry at Sedgebrook, show us that these age-groups defy the stereotypes often associated with them—youth as being uninterested in spiritual life and elder adults as being rigid in their beliefs. If your congregation is one, like many, that is missing one or more generations in your membership, I hope these stories inspire you to look beyond what you do not have and to discover the untapped creative energy in your congregation.

The story of Mary and Elizabeth, which opened the chapter, reminds us that all generations have special roles. Each contributes unique wisdom to the body of Christ. We are called upon mutually to find our gifts and resources and to "encourage one another and build up each other" (1 Thess. 5:11).

CHAPTER FIVE

Inviting the Spirit into
PRAYER GROUPS

There are varieties of gifts, but the same Spirit;
and there are varieties of services, but the same Lord;
and there are varieties of activities, but it is the
same God who activates all of them in everyone. To each
is given the manifestation of the Spirit for the common good.
—1 Corinthians 12:4-7

IN HER BOOK *A Praying Congregation,* Jane Vennard describes a variety of ways in which congregations manifest their desire for a deeper relationship with God through prayer:

> A praying congregation responds to people's longing to pray and their experiences and questions about prayer. The church prepares members' hearts so they are able to receive new information about specific prayer forms and spiritual practices and discover ways to integrate this knowledge into their daily lives. As individuals and groups seek to deepen their relationship with God they may request guidance about a particular method of prayer. Maybe they have heard about centering prayer and want to know what it is and how to do it. Others might be interested in more informal ways to pray and ask for instruction. Members of a prayer chain or some other structure for prayers of intercession may desire ongoing instruction and encouragement.[1]

In this chapter we will hear from several people who have found unique ways of teaching prayer and creating groups that foster deep sharing together. People are inviting the Spirit into their prayer lives and their congregations with use of the prayer labyrinth, Centering Prayer, prayer walks in nature, artistic expression in images, and a myriad of other practices. Patricia Brown's *Paths to Prayer* guides the reader through forty different prayer forms, drawn from Christian tradition. Stating that "one size doesn't fit all," she invites readers to explore "searching prayer," "experiential prayer," "relational prayer," and "innovative prayer" forms.[2] A prayer renaissance is underway in Christian life today. The stories that follow give a glimpse into what happens in churches small and large when people follow the creative Spirit to renew hearts through prayer and reflection together.

SPIRITUAL FORMATION GROUP COVENANTS

PEOPLE TODAY ARE captivated by the image of celebrity leadership and the megachurch phenomenon. In measuring success by big numbers, we have managed to downplay the importance of people meeting together in twos and threes. Today's infatuation with ministry to the masses is not scriptural. Yes, Jesus does address large numbers—in the feeding of the five thousand, for example. Yet we read many more stories of his encounters with individuals.

I am indebted to Tom Albin's insight in a lecture in which he pointed out that Jesus models three kinds of encounters for us: (1) to individuals; (2) to the small group of intimates, the Twelve; (3) and to the masses.[3] Following this model, let me suggest that spiritual formation ministries can foster: (1) individual spiritual direction, (2) small-group spiritual formation, (3) congregation-wide spiritual formation. As the stories in this book demonstrate, many people are experiencing an individual awakening in their spiritual life. We have also read about creative ways for worship, ministry with the "masses." Now we explore the second type of encounter—in small groups. First are accounts of two covenanted women's groups, from Eugenia Gamble at First Presbyterian Church in Birmingham, Alabama, and then from Helen Stegall in Arkansas:

> Since the early centuries of the Christian church when the women of the Aventine Hill in Rome met in each other's homes for scripture study and prayer, women have been drawn together for small groups of support and spiritual deepening. Whether it was sewing or quilting groups in which women prayed with their stitches or harp circles where women played and danced their joys and laments; whether in gatherings

for learning or for doing, women are simply different in same-gender groups. For many, those groups are as vital as breath.

The Women's Spirituality Group at First Church began shortly after I arrived as pastor. In the beginning we formed ourselves into a small and close-knit community by studying Ron DelBene's workbook *The Hunger of the Heart*. The group met weekly for one and one-half hours together. By the time we finished that workbook, we had developed our own pattern.

We spent time deciding exactly what type of group we were and made some important commitments to each other. Here is an excerpt from our group covenant: "This group is not a Bible study group, although the Bible is often our primary text. We are not a support group, although we experience incredible support. We are not an encounter group or a therapy group, although we may sometimes confront each other and often receive insights and healing. *We are a spiritual development group.* Our purpose is to grow in our relationship with God and to experience that relationship both personally and in the context of a small community set apart for that purpose. We do not do this work alone because the biblical way is always the way of community. God calls a people and works salvation in the midst of a people. The goal is both individual and group transformation. In the end it is God who is forming this group. It is, really, only God who can make a community of ragtag, bobtail, fearful humanity."

Once our group settled on our purpose and ground rules, we developed a pattern of daily spiritual practice. It was a simple pattern of reflection and journal writing. We also randomly drew names for weekly prayer companions. These pairs connected during the week for prayer and support.

Our weekly meeting process was simple as well. Members, grounded with spiritual reading and practice during the week, began each meeting by lighting the Christ candle and sharing requests for prayer. This also became a time of checking in and deep connection. For the next thirty to forty-five minutes we discussed a book we were reading together or heard a presentation from a member. We then shared insights and struggles from the week. We closed each meeting with twenty minutes of candlelight Evening Prayer in the small chapel of our church. Whenever we finished a book or study topic, we opened the group to new members and carefully took the time to get new members thoroughly incorporated into the group.

One of the most meaningful series for us was a study of the ancient women martyrs, mystics, and reformers. As we learned from these women's stories, we began to feel a much deeper connection to the long stream of women's Christian history and experience. Along the way, remarkable transformation took place.

The group was still in existence nine years later when I left the church to answer a new call. During the years when we met together weekly, the faces changed from time to time. Women moved in and out of the group depending on their circumstances. We celebrated the birth of babies, the emptying of nests, the finding of true love, and the loss of dreams in divorce. We rode the tides of depression, confusion, losing and finding our voices. Throughout it all we found ourselves pulled by the Spirit out of the oh-so-American spirit of individualism and isolation into a truer expression of unity and community. It was not always a smooth ride. We did not always incorporate new members easily. We sometimes welcomed women into the group who did not work out, and we were left to deal with the confusion and guilt associated with the ragged aspects of community.

I have been gone from the group for nearly seven years now, Still, every Thursday evening, I feel a spark of loss, gratitude, and longing for what that group meant to me.

Another women's group began with a study of personality types, the Enneagram, and prayer styles. Helen Stegall tells their story:

Group spiritual direction has been a part of my calling to vocation for a long time. In the spring of 2011, I began meeting with a group of eight women for spiritual direction and discernment. The group evolved out of women's retreats held in 2009 and 2010.

The church I serve has offered twenty women's retreats over a twelve-year period. The retreats' activities encourage self-reflection and awareness, as well as providing some informational content. In 2009 we used the Keirsey-Bates Temperament Sorter and held individual spiritual direction sessions with the participants as a tool for self-understanding. For many of the participants, it was their first experience of considering how personality affects worship, prayer style preference, and ways of imaging God.

The following year, based on the success of using personality inventory as a spiritual tool, we offered an introduction to the Enneagram. About seventy women attended that retreat, and many told me they wanted to learn more about the Enneagram. Their interest prompted me to lead a five-week class based on resources from Richard Rohr and Russ Hudson. Twelve women attended the class. At the end of the five weeks, I asked them to be in prayer about continuing to meet for small-group spiritual direction. Eight women eagerly agreed to continue. At this point the group became a closed group for the sake of confidentiality and to accommodate the interior work we do together.

The group meets weekly for one and one-half hours in homes. The atmosphere in a home setting is more conducive to the kind of deep sharing that occurs, and the spiritual gift of hospitality becomes part of our offering to one another. The spirit of place matters in awakening to the movement of God's presence in our lives. Responsibilities are shared among group members, so it is a leaderless group. The format includes an opening, individual check-in, a presentation for reflection, silence, response to the presentation, silent prayer, and a time of closing. We rotate the roles required to support the format: Opener, Hospitality, Presenter, Time Keeper, Closer. Perhaps the most difficult role is Time Keeper. No one readily volunteers to keep us moving through the schedule, but we agree that this element is essential to keeping us accountable to one another and to the process of attention to and awareness of the Spirit moving through our lives.

Participants report several benefits: the community and companionship with others seeking a closer relationship with God, receiving encouragement, practicing holy listening, intentional silence and time for reflection, trust and support for sharing feelings and struggles, clarifying spiritual history and experiences, understanding that we are different and learning from that difference, affirming the importance of self-awareness for drawing closer to God and to others, and developing discernment of the Holy Spirit's activity in our lives.

Clergy in local congregations often face a challenge in finding community where our own spirits are nurtured, encouraged, and supported. Forming this group has allowed me to participate with some of my congregation members in mutual spiritual support. At our first session I arrived wearing a clerical collar. When it was my time to check in, I removed the collar as a ritual way of saying, "I am one of you now, not your pastor in this setting." My hope is that I am offering a role model for them, in that clergy are also "pilgrims on the way," human beings needing companionship and community for the journey.

These two stories reveal the exceptional presence to one another created in small-group spiritual direction practice. Are we not experiencing the fruit of the Spirit together—"love, joy, peace, patience, kindness, generosity, faithfulness, gentleness, and self-control" (Gal. 5:22-23)? Other prayer practices, such as Centering Prayer, walking the prayer labyrinth, praying through art expression, and walking in nature, also can give rise to these fruits of the Spirit.

CENTERING PRAYER GROUP

THE PURPOSE OF Centering Prayer is to meditate on God's love using a simple word or phrase to keep the mind focused. Based on the fourteenth-century English text *The Cloud of Unknowing*, it recalls the mystery of the cloud as found in many places in scripture. Moses goes into the cloud on Mount Sinai when receiving the Ten Commandments. Jesus enters the cloud in the moment of the Transfiguration, in which he is seen to be in the company of Elijah and Moses. The cloud image signifies approaching the mystery of God directly.

Profound work can take place when we bring all our thoughts to God in a spirit of redeeming love. This prayer practice has been taught widely through the work of Basil Pennington and Thomas Keating and the organization Contemplative Outreach.[4] Here Mary Hooper relates the ups and downs with group experience in Centering Prayer at Central United Methodist Church in Meridian, Mississippi:

> The first time I centered, I was hooked. It was like a floodgate had been opened up, and I was awash with a new, deeper spirituality. Centering Prayer met a need and desire in me so powerfully that it has changed my life. I had a hunger for a different kind of prayer-filled life, a richer, fuller practice of the presence of God. My Centering Prayer practice of twenty minutes twice a day has become part of who I am and has fulfilled the longing. It helps me feel that I am a beloved child of God, something I knew for many years.
>
> My personal spiritual journey had progressed through prayer and devotional/study time. My corporate spiritual journey had been filled with teaching and volunteering in any and all capacities of my local United Methodist church. But the second half of life brought change. New friendships sparked new spiritual adventures.

I had attended a Contemplative Outreach–sponsored workshop at my local church. A weekly Centering Prayer group formed. The community of seekers began to open doors to new realms of possibilities. Centering Prayer is what I had yearned for in my personal spiritual journey.

The next spring, another Centering Prayer workshop was organized at my local church by our small group. A small core group of committed individuals continued to meet regularly. We studied the Contemplative Outreach follow-up videos *Six Continuing Sessions of the Introduction to the Centering Prayer Practice* and others.[5] The next year we offered another Contemplative Outreach Centering Prayer workshop, followed by a small-group meeting. We studied a new DVD series *Invitation from God*. Yet, our small group eventually disbanded. Our associate pastor, who had been very supportive, moved away, and participation had declined. I am sorry to report that the only other small prayer group nearby, at an Episcopal church, also disbanded.

After a hiatus of some months, Mary reported that the weekly group had started again at her congregation. She ponders the ups and downs of sustaining the group:

What happened? After offering the Centering Prayer workshop three times at our church (with over thirty at each workshop), we still found it difficult to form and sustain a small group. Finding a time that a group could commit to was as challenging as getting people to commit to a weekly meeting. But the main issue was a lack of interest in the contemplative tradition. In a society that values to-do lists and noise, it would seem that silence, solitude, and resting in God are too foreign. Whether it is lack of knowledge of the contemplative tradition or the Southern Protestant culture that is prejudiced against anything suspiciously Catholic or new age, Centering Prayer has had a difficult time sustaining a weekly group meeting in Meridian, Mississippi. Despite growth and education, most people still view Centering Prayer as a unique, new, or nontraditional practice.

Whether supported by the small group or not, my personal practice of Centering Prayer has grown. Forgiveness for myself and for others was one of the first healings I began to experience. Learning to love myself as God does has helped me to really love others. My twice-daily practice of Centering Prayer has opened me up to allow God to uplift,

inspire, and guide me more than ever before. Most of all, it has allowed
God to begin to heal and continue to heal the broken parts of me.

Mary Hooper's story suggests that spiritual formation work is pioneering. "The wind blows where it chooses, and you hear the sound
of it, but you do not know where it comes from or where it goes. So
it is with everyone who is born of the Spirit" (John 3:8). As people
introduce contemplative practices, they must be willing to risk expla-
nations to their congregations and accept that groups may sustain
themselves for a while but then perhaps end or change forms.

PRAYER LABYRINTH

A MEDIEVAL FORM of prayer, the labyrinth has come into prominence
again as a walking prayer practice since the early 1990s. Through the
vision of Rev. Dr. Lauren Artress, this practice has been rediscovered
after dormancy in the West of at least five hundred years. Labyrinth
patterns arose throughout Europe around 1200 CE, during a period
of high devotion and pilgrimage. The pattern on the floor of Chartres
Cathedral in Chartres, France, has become the most well known of
these patterns.

In medieval times, Chartres Cathedral was one among numerous cathedrals designated as pilgrimage destinations for Christians
in Europe. At one time, European Christians had expected to make
a pilgrimage to Jerusalem at least once in their life, but the wars of
the Crusades made travel too dangerous, so pilgrimage cathedrals
became the alternative. One could fulfill the obligation of pilgrimage
by going to one of these designated sites rather than to Jerusalem.
We can only imagine the sense of divine encounter that occurred for
people who were otherwise leading meager lives as they stepped into
a magnificent cathedral, saw the stories of the Bible come alive in
stained-glass windows, heard the sounds of chanting, and perhaps
walked the labyrinth for a time of inspiration.

Today people find walking a labyrinth to be a profound form of
prayer. In her book *Walking a Sacred Path,* Lauren Artress outlines the
process as a means of moving through the classic steps of Christian
prayer: (1) *purgation,* letting go of our assumptions and concerns, as

we walk into the labyrinth; (2) *illumination,* as we receive inspiration at the center; and (3) *union* of our experience with life concerns as we walk out of the labyrinth and back into our daily lives.[6]

In the following account, Marjorie Donnelly describes the creation of a 365-day prayer calendar at Holy Trinity Episcopal Church in Greensboro, North Carolina:

The Holy Trinity Labyrinth Keepers, an ecumenical group of sixteen members, provides education and facilitates walks on Holy Trinity's outdoor labyrinth. We are sponsored and financially supported by the church. In 2008, we launched a project with the goal of a 365-day presence on the labyrinth at Holy Trinity Episcopal Church.

Our inspiration came from the Labyrinth Society's 365 Club Daily Walkers, whose members each commit to walking a labyrinth somewhere in the world every day for a year. Rather than each individual walking every day, we have at least one person walk Holy Trinity's labyrinth every day. This approach fulfills our desire for a community-building project for Holy Trinity and an outreach to the Greensboro community. People from different walks of life and different faith traditions can share in the commitment to keep the energy of peace and love flowing on a

daily basis by walking the Holy Trinity labyrinth. Walkers pray for one another and for peace in the community and the world as they walk.

Holy Trinity's labyrinth is located in a cloistered and well-lighted outdoor space adjacent to the sanctuary. Walkers may choose any time of the day that is most convenient for them to walk. An online calendar allows people to sign up easily. People may commit to walk as often as they want, and there is no limit to the number of people walking on a given day. Some individuals walk one or more days a week; others walk monthly or once a year. That single day might be the walker's birthday, anniversary, or another special day. Some people sign up for the same day and time each week or each month. On occasion, groups walk the labyrinth together as a bonding activity for work teams, covenant groups, even book clubs. If a person cannot keep a commitment to walk on a certain day, using a finger labyrinth at home or simply praying is an acceptable alternative.

Quarterly support circles for the 365 Club Daily Walkers provide opportunities to share individual labyrinth experiences as well as for the whole group to walk together. Participants in the project report a number of benefits: (1) experiencing a kind of body prayer that quiets your mind, allowing the spirit to become receptive to the still small voice of God; (2) practicing walking meditation and "putting feet on your prayers"; (3) encouraging insight and self-reflection; (3) facilitating creativity and celebration; (4) finding a closer walk with God; (5) praying for others and our world and a sense of community, knowing that others are also praying for you; and (6) praying for peace.

Once, Holy Trinity's beautiful eleven-circuit Chartres-style stone labyrinth was underutilized. Now, when you pass by, you more than likely will see a labyrinth walker or a group walking and praying together. Nearby, a replica of the Muiredach Celtic high cross bears witness to this sacred place. Prayer is central to our life together as Christians. The 365 day labyrinth walkers are a visible sign to the Holy Trinity community and beyond of prayer's central focus in our communal life. As the cross bears witness to the sacred, so the walkers also bear witness to the cross. It is a quiet ministry that I believe transforms lives one step at a time.

Glynden Bode from Houston, Texas, describes how a small prayer group walks for peace:

Here is an account of a few women who set out to walk the labyrinth for peace in response to events of the day that seemed incongruent with the life and teachings of Jesus. Within the labyrinth community in the area, word and invitation went out, and four women responded. In the fall of 2002, the drums of war were beating steadily, daily growing louder and stronger and faster it seemed. We asserted that war is incompatible with Christian teaching; war is antithetical to the gospel of Christ; war causes immense harm to the world community (relationships, nations), to creation (bombing, minefields, burning, destroying, polluting), to individual souls (taking the life of another human being, acts of desperation for economic means, acts of betrayal for self-preservation); war cannot be a part of the realm of God, for it is a profound form of brokenness; war is not part of God's plan.

With these thoughts in our hearts and minds, this ecumenical group of women began to meet monthly, to walk the labyrinth, and to share. We joined together to circle the path of the labyrinth for peace.

We sought to visualize another reality, God's reality. Prayer is a way of seeing a different reality, a different way of being with others in the world. We longed to see through God's eyes, not human eyes, and to claim an alternative reality that reflected the gospel of Christ, the realm of God, the shalom of God—for all.

In expressing our intention for gathering, we affirmed our belief that all persons are formed in the image of God, that there is a "God-spark" in each one, and thus great potential for the human community to live into God's shalom. We chose the labyrinth because we knew it to be a remarkable spiritual tool for clarity, discernment, healing, peace, creativity, and new life. As we walked, we were seeing with God an alternative vision. This was a countercultural action, as are many spiritual acts of faith. The drums of war were beating in the background and even in the church. In the context of the faith community in Houston, Texas, our actions were definitely "coloring outside the lines."

Our format was simple. We would gather and check in with one another. As led, individuals would share a piece of scripture or other spiritual writing, a poem, an image, an object—followed by silent reflection. This provided our spark for that time together. Sharing our reflections led to agreement upon a question with which to walk. (One example: "What is the fear that drives our nation?") Then we walked the labyrinth, and we processed our experiences with art and journaling.

Finally, we shared our experiences on the path, our Spirit-moments, the wisdom we were offered and received. We were together about three hours each time we met, and we always departed with great hope, wonder, and a profound sense of Presence. We had become vulnerable to Love and sought Love's alternative reality for all.

INTENTIONAL WALKS IN NATURE

YET ANOTHER FORM of prayer walking is described by Nancy Rowe.[7] These intentional walks are held in settings of natural beauty:

> Recently I spent time at a retreat center. A group of teenagers accompanied by their parish priest were there at the same time. One night, hearing rustling feet and noticing lights outside my window, I discovered these teenagers walking silently together with their priest in the moonlit night. Each had a flashlight to illuminate the path.
>
> Intrigued, the following morning I asked a sixteen-year-old what the group was doing. She responded, "We were taking a walk that reminds us that we each have a light inside and that we are to shine our own light in the world." I was stunned by the clarity and spiritual maturity of this explanation and how, through this experience in nature, a young person understood more about becoming a spiritual light in the world. By embodying this wisdom teaching, she perceived the essence of her own spirituality—her own inner light—and also experienced her connection with the natural world. This was truly a "walking prayer."
>
> This anecdote illustrates the impact that being in collaboration with nature can have on our spiritual awareness as well as our sense of who we are within our earth community. I am on the faculty of a spiritual-based graduate program and deeply inspired by the work of Thomas Berry. I feel called to create opportunities for others to connect consciously with nature and, more importantly, to experience being part of the natural world. People long for this connection; I have seen them cry as they read the poems they create after spending time in nature. I have seen people soothe their grief by creating gardens and walking silently on the land while observing the cycles of life. This deep connection with earth is vital to the human spirit.
>
> I provide opportunities for this connection by facilitating "intentional walks" that people can do individually or in groups. These walks allow

people to connect directly with the ensouled landscape and with themselves as human beings living in the cosmos. The walks are "intentional" in that they provide participants time and space to open up to specific spiritual qualities, such as gratitude, spiritual relationship, appreciation, reverence, wonder, awe, and beauty. These qualities promote appreciation of the interconnection of all beings.

These walks are invented or adapted from various wisdom traditions. For example, a walk called "Bowing to the Spirit" is adapted from a walk passed down by Thich Nhat Hanh. In this thirty-minute experience participants walk contemplatively in a natural setting relatively free of interruption. They begin by setting an intention of being in relationship with or feeling part of the natural world. I suggest that they walk slowly and mindfully and feel the ground beneath their feet. Every few minutes the walkers stop and notice their surroundings. They look in all directions, taking in the landscape with all their senses. After a short time, they continue walking slowly, consciously, noting with expanded awareness and appreciation the trees, animals, insects, plants, and other humans with whom they share the land. They stop periodically and mark the end of their walk with a prayer, poem, or an expression of gratitude.

When I guide this walk, I begin with an activity that opens participants to all of their senses. I then invite them to be aware that they are a human community walking in relationship with one another within the natural world. I remind them to experience their human connection to their living landscape. I read a nature poem or prayer and then begin this silent walk. Periodically, I ring a bell as a cue for participants to pause, open their awareness, and take in their surroundings. We pause at least seven times on the walk. Generally, the walk ends at a place of great beauty. We close with another nature poem or prayer.

Another walk is based on *The Soul's Journey into God* by Bonaventure, who invited us to observe nature through our senses and ask, *What does this experience tell me about God?*[8]

These walks can shift participants' consciousness. Once I asked a group to find something in nature that they considered "ordinary." After gazing at it for a while, I asked them to see it as "extraordinary." One person who had been on intentional walks with me before exclaimed, "Nancy, last year I could have done this, but now I can no longer see the natural world as 'ordinary.'"

CONTEMPLATIVE ART

ONE OF THE most significant prayer forms in Christian tradition is using our inner senses to imagine scripture stories, a process particularly identified with the *Spiritual Exercises of Saint Ignatius*.[9] Ignatius asks us to enter stories in the Bible by experiencing the text through each sense—hearing, seeing, smelling, tasting, touching. This approach makes scripture come alive in our imaginations, enabling us to relate the scripture to our own lives. Artist and writer Karla Kincannon explains how contemplative art practices also employ our senses to enhance spiritual growth:

Contemplative art practices enable individuals to grow in their knowledge of God and knowledge of self, strengthening them for their faith journey. Individuals participating in contemplative art practices or *art from the soul* frequently express surprise at the deep meaning and sense of peace they experience. New energies for living often follow the making of *art from the soul*. When groups experience this prayer practice, community is nourished and spiritual friendships are formed. Using contemplative creative practices in congregations assists in awakening the movement of the Holy Spirit within the body of Christ and brings new vitality to the faith community.

Susan had not painted since the third grade. When she participated in an *art from the soul* weekend retreat at her church, she discovered she was fed as she used her creativity. Following the retreat, she enrolled in art classes, adding a new dimension to her life.

Jamal received clear direction while creating *art from the soul*. Spiritually he had been burdened by an unforgiving spirit, holding a grudge against a family member because of a previous wound. During an experience of painting his grudge, he reframed the experience of the original wound and moved closer to healing.

Cynthia's prayer group decided to study *Creativity and Divine Surprise: Finding the Place of Your Resurrection*, a book I authored. The book's creative exercises opened her to new experiences of God's love and peace. Despite the turmoil in her life, she found assurance of God's abiding presence in the midst of a horrific divorce.

At Grace United Methodist Church, artists came out of the woodwork after a weekend retreat on *art from the soul*. The church formed an arts ministry, which led to a series of art shows in the fellowship hall. Art became a tool for evangelism in that congregation.

While these vignettes describe the experiences of adults, *art from the soul* also works well with youth, young adults, and older adults. Although artistic expression is normally associated with the very young or with professional artists, it is open to everyone. We are made in the image of a great Creator, making us all artists of one kind or another. Awakening our creativity enables us to live into the fullness of the image of God within each of us. Using art as a prayer practice guides us to encounter God and provides a means of expression for the soul. The goal of *art from the soul* is not a pretty picture. The focus is the process. *Art from the soul* is created with the nondominant hand, a technique that reaches the innermost part of the self as well as offering a way to listen for the voice of God.

Using the nondominant hand lessens fear about trying this spiritual exercise for the first time. It gives generous permission to create art in which the product remains unimportant. The participant/artist becomes free to listen for both the voice of the soul and the voice of God. *Art from the soul* is an excellent tool for discernment. Many pieces created with this method are stunning in their power, beauty, and revelation; all have a childlike quality. Participants become like little children to whom the kingdom of God belongs. The process encourages vulnerability akin to that of children and the vulnerability of the prayer experience. An atmosphere of safety and trust fosters support for the exploration of the soul, development of community, and nurture of spiritual friendships.

I have introduced contemplative art practices to congregations in two ways: (1) leading a weekend retreat with an open invitation to all members, and (2) working within an existing covenant group whose members desired to deepen their spirituality through exploration of the arts. As a spiritual director, I have used *art from the soul* with directees in individual sessions. Whether in small or large groups or in individual sessions, the results are similar. God speaks to people in profound ways through contemplative art practices.

Exercises for exploring creativity as prayer are included in *Creativity and Divine Surprise* and in *Awakening the Creative Spirit: Bringing the Arts to Spiritual Direction* by Christine Valters Paintner and Betsey Beckman. I lead individuals into an art experience with a guided meditation or an experience of *lectio divina*. Then I invite participants to draw what they feel, sense, or intuit, listening for an awareness, hunch, or gut feeling to direct them where to place color on the paper. The entire time of creating becomes one of listening to the Holy Spirit for guidance in placing paint on paper. A period of silent prayer is recommended before beginning to create.

When we use our God-given creativity as a contemplative practice, the creative Spirit of God comes to us in new and exciting ways, empowering us for the life God intends us to lead.

A related artistic process is collage. Like the use of the nondominant hand described by Karla Kincannon, collage cuts through the art inhibitions many people have. Everyone can tear out pictures from magazines. Collage can be introduced with scripture meditation focusing on a story, such as Jesus' encounter with the man lame for thirty-eight years, asking, "Do you want to be made well?" (John 5:6). Or the theme can be posed as a question such as, "What is God asking of you now in your life?" The *art from the soul* principles show us why the group discernment process described in chapter 3 works so well. The sensory-rich images from John 15 of the vine and the branches stir the imagination for discernment of corporate mission. I was introduced to collage more than twenty years ago and cherish the collage journals I have produced through the years. The process is useful during times of discernment of major life changes. Images appear in unexpected ways that help to articulate latent hopes.

TAKING MEN TO A DEEPER LEVEL

FINALLY, LET'S LOOK at ways for men to invite the Spirit into small groups. The ratio of women to men who contributed to this book suggests that more women than men engage in prayer. While this may be true of twentieth-century and twenty-first-century Western Christians, it has not been true historically. Over the years men as well as women have embraced contemplative prayer practices. Remember how many historic figures responsible for renewing Christian prayer have been men. One of the best ways I have found to engage men in prayer is by exploring the four themes articulated by N. Graham Standish in *Forming Faith in a Hurricane: A Spiritual Primer for Daily Living.*

Standish describes prayer in four different modes: prayer as thinking, prayer as loving, prayer as listening, and prayer as speaking. It is very refreshing for men to be asked how they primarily ponder their lives. Many men are thinkers. They think carefully and systematically, but they may not have recognized such pondering as a prayer process. Others move straight into action, which Standish calls prayer as loving. Reflection takes place in the midst of activity and service. The contemplative prayer forms we've been describing fall into the listening mode. Active prayer forms are forms of speaking our prayers. We are made for prayer. We are made to ponder life fully and deeply. We simply may not have a wide enough definition of prayer. Many men also report the importance of being in nature as they fish or hunt. The capture of fish or wild game may not be as important as the opportunity for a heightened sensory experience of a day apart, in which people experience profound relationship with nature.

Todd Smiedendorf creates opportunities for men to reflect in a wilderness experience:

> It was over ten years ago that I experienced a life-altering men's retreat. While the retreat was not explicitly Christian, I recognized the gospel as deeply implicit in this way of retreat. It should be called an ancient-future way of Spirit, drawing on ancient sources and practices and weaving them together with new ways, a powerful mix of wilderness setting, group council, ancient ritual, and personal process. What inspired me was the experiential depth, the powerful energetic of soul that was present. This was the beginning of the annual summer camp CrossRoads in the Wilderness: Reconnecting Men, God and Earth. I wanted to make this way of men's retreat explicitly Christian so men around the church could access this kind of retreat.
>
> It took some years of further retreats doing staffing, being mentored, and being trained, before CrossRoads could be made real. I found other Christian-identified men who had experienced this way of retreat who were interested in helping. Our CrossRoads leadership team has been composed of men with experience in this kind of retreat and has varied from three to five, each having responsibility for some area of the retreat. I found a location at a rustic, remote church-owned camp. Experience taught us that a Thursday night through Sunday midday schedule was a

workable compromise of enough time for benefit and not so much time that men would not give it a try.

This is the recipe that gives CrossRoads its potency: (1) retreating to a wilderness setting to bring men closer to creation in its less civilized forms; (2) creating a safe place to listen to each other's stories in group settings; (3) providing a manual to give background to the underlying understandings, the expectations, and the setting; (4) using influence of First Nation sensibilities; (5) inviting participation in two ancient rituals common to most cultures (sweat prayer and solo fast); (6) facilitating personal growth and breakthroughs through "carpet work" (a kind of ritual psychodrama); and (7) engaging in an art project in which participants take away the energy and learning of the retreat in a concrete symbolic form (such as making a shield, staff, and so forth).

The biggest hurdle was communicating the vision to potential participants. It took time to spread the word and develop the trust necessary for men to commit to something new and untried. This retreat format is experiential and unusual. In some ways, it cannot be described as much as experienced.

Now that we have done several CrossRoads in the Wilderness retreats, I know it was worth the effort. This kind of retreat was life-altering when I first encountered it, liberating me to love and to feel more confident, more clear, more connected to men, creation, and Spirit. I was able to deal with old hurts and issues, allowing grace to enter in. It has renewed my hope for the world to see men do this soul work together, to see what is possible, and to feel the presence of Spirit.

CrossRoads past participants say: "This work made it possible to enter the heartwork that I have difficulty entering. The location, leadership, and structure made it possible." "I learned to be more balanced. Renewed the love I have for myself and the things I love to do." "Gave me the space to explore the Spirit and expand my soul." "Important to me for maintaining perspective and a connection with who I am, who I want to be and what is essential in life. The real connection to other men is something that I desire, but rarely find in other settings."

I encourage participants to read these three books: *King, Warrior, Magician, Lover: Rediscovering the Archetypes of the Mature Masculine* by Robert Moore and Douglas Gillette; *Adam's Return: The Five Promises of Male Initiation* by Richard Rohr; and *4Gateways Coaching* by Tom Daly.

• • •

In this chapter, we have learned several ways in which the Holy Spirit is acting among us through prayer and reflection. Certainly not every prayer practice will be something to adopt in your situation, but they may give you a creative nudge to move into some new forms of prayer and service. Remember, there are "many gifts, one Spirit."

In his book *Sacred Pathways: Discover Your Soul's Path to God,* Gary Thomas names nine ways individuals may express and experience loving God: (1) naturalists: loving God out of doors; (2) sensates: loving God with the senses; (3) traditionalists: loving God through ritual and symbol; (4) ascetics: loving God in solitude and simplicity; (5) activists: loving God through confrontation; (6) caregivers: loving God by loving others; (7) enthusiasts: loving God with mystery and celebration; (8) contemplatives: loving God through adoration; (9) intellectuals: loving God with the mind. Stories in this chapter came from naturalists, sensates, ascetics, and contemplatives. Each points to the great mystery of God.

If you are thinking through spiritual formation ministry in your congregation and community, now may be a good time to study some of the different prayer forms in more detail. You'll find suggested resources in the small-group guide at the back of the book.

CHAPTER SIX

Inviting the Spirit into
SPIRITUAL LIFE MINISTRIES

Jesus said to them,
"I am the bread of life.
Whoever comes to me will never be hungry,
and whoever believes in me will never be thirsty."
—John 6:35

LIFEHOUSE MINISTRY IN Ruston, Louisiana, describes itself as a "ministry portal or door into deeper life with God. It is a supplement for the church, a place through which a soul can journey to find its worth and to have others spiritually companion him or her along the way." Cherri Johnson was named director of spiritual formation at First United Methodist Church in Baton Rouge, Louisiana, "a ministry little known or understood within the congregation. The language and practice of spiritual formation and spiritual direction were nonexistent. They did not exist in the consciousness or ethos of the community. I realized at that time that I was starting 'at square one.'" Saint Luke's United Methodist Church in Indianapolis, Indiana, was inspired by "the dream of a task force that wanted in-church programming similar to what was available at retreat centers." Congregations are beginning to name a spiritual director in residence.

Many congregations are developing a unique focus in spiritual formation, often through the inspired leadership of a single individual. Spiritual formation is a new ministry area for the twenty-first-century church yet deeply steeped in Christian history. These efforts align with the movement for spiritual depth that has been awakening in the church for the past thirty years. As early as the mid-1990s, the language of spiritual formation was becoming common enough that Christian Schwarz named "passionate spirituality" as one of the eight constituent elements of vital congregations in *Natural Church Development: A Guide to Eight Essential Qualities of Healthy Churches.* United Methodist Bishop Robert Schnase included "intentional faith development" as one of the *Five Practices of Fruitful Congregations.*

These same themes are named in the purpose of eighteenth-century Methodist societies: "a company of [people] having the *form* and seeking the *power* of godliness, united in order to pray together, to receive the word of exhortation, and to watch over one another in love, that they may help each other to work out their salvation."[1] We are rediscovering the power of God's grace mediated through prayer and small-group faith sharing. We are learning again how to "watch over one another in love." While prayer is not new, the panoply of prayer forms being widely taught is new. While the need for deep conversations with others about matters of faith and life is not new, the range of resources available to facilitate this conversation is new. This novelty means that bringing spiritual formation practices into the center of congregational and community life remains pioneering work.

LEAVEN IN THE BREAD OF JESUS CHRIST

CHERRI JOHNSON SHARES some of the challenges in bringing a spiritual life center to reality at First United Methodist Church in Baton Rouge, Louisiana:

> In truth, there was little pastoral support in the initial stages of ministry development. Our senior pastor was focused on education, evangelism, and service. But as the ministry flourished and grew, he became more supportive and affirming. The initial years of development were hard on me emotionally. With little affirmation, I had to rely on God and developing my own inner strength and resiliency. Fortunately, I had established a faith community beyond the walls of the local church. Mentors and spiritual directors encouraged and supported me and held me accountable. I still find these individuals and groups to be most instrumental and important in my own maturation.

After eight years of faithful service in this ministry, Cherri Johnson describes profound results within the congregation:

The ministry of spiritual formation is becoming the leaven in the Bread of Jesus Christ—gradually forming and shaping the culture and ethos of our congregation. We are raising up *spiritual* leaders and empowering them in their calling. The ministry provides the container for a committed core group to delve deeper into spiritual practice. We are enabling members to reach out into the world and become agents of God's redemptive, saving grace.

As we hear in this chapter from people who have been developing such a focus within their congregations and communities, we will discover a common process that has been fruitful. People listen for needs and respond. They discover skills and interests of others and bring them forth. Developing a spiritual formation focus becomes leavening of the Spirit within the larger body of Christ. Like those present at the first Pentecost, people are hearing the message of God's grace with their hearts, "each one in their own language." Cherri Johnson tells more about how this ministry is developing:

I began to offer that which I knew best—one-on-one spiritual direction, contemplative worship experiences, walking and praying the labyrinth. Only a few people attended, and sometimes I simply "held the space" for God. However, some wanted to know more. They would ask: "What is this ministry all about? What is spiritual direction?" I responded, "When are you free? How about meeting for coffee?"

I began to notice the deep hunger and need placed right before me—the young father who wanted to parent as a more committed Christian; the young man who wanted to know more about spiritual direction; the women who were hungry for spiritual renewal. As I listened with the "ears of my heart," God revealed the way. I offered classes on the language of spiritual formation—*Exploring the Way, The Way of Blessedness, The Way of Discernment*, all from the Companions in Christ series. I offered book studies on the saints and mystics, including contemporary authors; and I began small-group spiritual direction. I publicized our many offerings in our newsletter.

A pilot group of young parents formed to explore Christian parenting in more depth and created a curriculum that included spiritual practice. I companioned a young man as he designed a curriculum for men. I began to offer spiritual life retreats. I assisted an older woman in bringing her heart's desire to life as we created a Life Mentoring (spiritual companioning) Ministry. In partnership with other denominations, the ministry brought in national speakers. The ministry began to offer opportunities for Centering Prayer and *lectio divina*. People responded positively; gradually and predictably, a "core group" formed. The spiritual hunger so evident in the beginning was now being satisfied.

From this beginning, a major ministry focus came into being:

Two years ago, by the grace of God, First United Methodist Church blessed and opened the doors to the Center for Spiritual Formation. The ministry of spiritual formation is now housed in a beautifully restored home situated next door to the main church building. Our programming and ministries are highly respected and are considered equal to all other ministry areas. We are now embarking on a mission to help our congregation understand how education (Bible study), outreach (mission), and spiritual formation (spiritual practice and prayer) are integral to the vitality of the church and how these three areas working together can transform the world. We will launch a new ministry of spiritual leadership, which we are calling Academy for Spiritual Leadership. This phase of ministry and discipleship is based on the Great Commandment, "Love the Lord your God with all your heart, and with all your soul, and with all your strength, and with all your mind; and your neighbor as yourself" (Luke 10:27).

It is essential that we, as the church, raise up more clergy and laity steeped in the practice of spiritual formation—accountable to their faith journey, with communities in which they can face their own shadow and do their deeper inner work. I believe this is the call placed on the emerging church—not simply addressing programmatic concerns but raising up and empowering spiritual leadership—clergy and laity committed to the deeper journey, leading others toward authentic transformation. This in turn will transform the world in which we live.

LEAVEN FOR THE WORLD

IN RUSTON, LOUISIANA, Cathy Brewton has brought a community-focused ministry of spiritual formation to life. LifeHouse Ministries has come about through sustained prayer and through visioning with a circle of friends. This ministry grows from Cathy Brewton's own sense of calling:

LifeHouse Ministries, Inc.,[2] is a nonprofit ministry of spiritual formation and healing, governed by a board of directors and advisory board. The vision for LifeHouse is to provide a presence of healing, hospitality, and reconciliation with God, neighbor, and self. Our desire is to enable persons to deepen their inner lives with God and become aware of God's presence in their everyday lives as a result of the opportunities that are offered.

The purpose of LifeHouse Ministries is to serve as a ministry portal or door into the kingdom of God offering sacred space, respite, and repose for persons who are spiritually impoverished, experiencing a faith crisis, or in need of healing. It is an ecumenical ministry open for all people to embark on the journey to wholeness in body, mind, and spirit. LifeHouse Ministries is a place to fabricate community and build relationships.

I am a United Methodist minister serving as a deacon in the church through my specialization in spiritual formation. I am called by God to move beyond the walls of the church into the world, to embody the grace and love of Jesus Christ to those pushed to the edges of our society, and to empower all persons to begin to see themselves as God's beloved. During my seminary journey of study, writing, meditation, and reflection, I began to have a vision for this place in the community, this house, for people to come and experience God in new and different ways. God has placed this ministry in my care and asked me to be the steward, the abbess for LifeHouse; and God desires for spiritual formation to be the centerpiece of all that we do in this sacred space.

Spiritual formation is a way of helping people to become aware of God in their physical journey so that God does not "stay inside the church," so to speak. It enables people to open up to the Spirit within them—the Divine Christ that dwells within us and moves among us. In our culture we tend to categorize our lives to the point of fragmentation. Spiritual formation enables us to become aware of God's presence when we are at work, at school, with our family and friends, and enjoying the beauty of God's creation in nature. LifeHouse Ministries is a neutral space in the community where people can come away from the hurried, busy, noisy world in which we live and into the quiet for rest and respite, in order to find restoration for their souls and to have a place to hear God.

Truly the beginnings of LifeHouse happened on the pages in my journal. Through prayer and listening, I began to gather board members; at our first meeting in the fall of 2009 we started the foundational work of this ministry. I worked with an attorney, a CPA, and the IRS to establish our nonprofit status and corporate name through the state of Louisiana. Our prayer as a board has always been to discern "the next thing" that God needs us to do in order not to become overwhelmed. We held our first fund-raising event in October 2010 and continue having big events once per year with smaller fund-raisers intermittently. At the first fund-raiser, a family offered a space for our ministry to be housed; the seed monies and monthly pledges acquired at that event gave us the means to use the space. We are located in the heart of the community surrounded by businesses and residences.

We currently offer prayer classes, organic gardening and horticultural therapy, and individual spiritual direction to help people with their relationship with God. We also offer spiritual movement classes accompanied by scripture reading or sacred music, so persons can embody the scriptures, hence the grace of our God. We offer space for healing ministries like Alcoholics Anonymous and Divorce Recovery.

LifeHouse offers clergy care for ministers in the community and surrounding communities and parishes. Ministers and pastors do not get a lot of quiet rest, so we provide space to them for quiet, meditation, and soul tending. Our hope is that they return to their families, churches, and places of ministry revitalized for ministry with God.

LifeHouse hosts community meals twice a month for anyone who wishes to sit together at the table. Jesus came to seek and save the lost. He came to remind us who we are and whose we are. Through his life we learn how to live and how to love each other. We always want to reach out to those in our community—those who are pushed to the margins. Meals together nurture reconciliation; masks come off and people see who they really are. Eating together and listening for God in each other's lives remind us that we are not alone, that we are one body of Christ.

LEAVEN IN CHURCH AND COMMUNITY

THE SPIRITUAL LIFE Center of Saint Luke's United Methodist Church in Indianapolis was conceived from its beginning, in the mid-1990s, as a resource for the congregation and the community. The program was envisioned at a time when remodeling of the church building allowed for creation of a prayer chapel adjacent to the outdoor columbarium. Space was also made available for a comfortable gathering room with a fireplace and artwork; it was designated as meeting space for the Spiritual Life Center. Betty Brandt has guided this ministry, first as part-time and now as full-time director. She describes enlisting people to utilize their own resources and gifts to design and offer programs with the Spiritual Life Center:[3]

One person with an established Christian meditation practice began an ongoing meditation group that continues today. Another individual, interested in how we listen for the "still small voice," offered intuition classes. A group of four women interested in hands-on healing received training in a healing modality called the Pilgrimage Healing Process, developed by an Episcopal priest. We now have a training center (over two hundred people from a variety of congregations have been trained) and an active healing ministry at Saint Luke's with an average of twenty appointments a month. A retired clergyman, intrigued with the spiritual messages in popular secular movies, initiated a Spiritual Cinema series.

Demand for body/mind/spirit opportunities led us to develop yoga, qigong, and aikido classes. We now have a labyrinth ministry, a green ministry, an art ministry, prayer vigils, outside speakers, and numerous classes. We openly honor and value progressive Christian theologians and authors. More than one hundred volunteers and paid instructors carry out the work of the Spiritual Life Center.

All our programming is open to the larger community, and more than half the people attending classes and events would not claim Saint Luke's as their church home. An e-mail list of more than two thousand receives our bimonthly program updates with complete listings and registration for classes on our website, and we maintain a Facebook page.

A twenty-member commission with a volunteer chair directs the work of the center based on a three-year long-range plan. There are three standing committees. The Development of the Inner Soul Committee turns its attention to the development of spiritual disciplines and special Advent and Lenten offerings. The External Connection Committee nurtures relationships with other congregations, faith communities, and cultural groups; it has hosted events with Buddhist, Native American, and Pakistani groups. The Infrastructure Committee works on publications, the library, and Internet opportunities (such as online classes). Many commission members have served for over ten years because they feel called to the work they are doing. The work of the Spiritual Life Center has had the support of clergy who desired experiential programming that included a focus on contemplation and spiritual disciplines. Traditional adult education offerings are managed by the director of adult education. Her programming has a cognitive and Bible-based focus.

My personal spiritual growth has been enormous since I began this journey in 1996 as an ordinary Methodist with a career background in marriage and family therapy. I surrounded myself with laypeople who introduced me to interesting ideas and practices. I was willing to trust and experiment to find out if people had a need or the desire to pursue these new avenues. People had meaningful spiritual experiences that they were hesitant to talk about; we wanted to provide a safe place and framework for those experiences to be shared and nurtured.

Any problems that arose in my eleven years as director were solved by a member of the Spiritual Life Center Commission. These individuals have been my sounding boards, my Facebook coaches, my time-management mentors, and my office/computer organizers. They know I can't do this job without them, and I value their brains, creativity, flexibility, prayers, and good humor. I see myself as the one who empowers others to develop and share their gifts. I do not provide any direct service. I am not clergy or a spiritual director; I am not trained in our healing modality. I am not a visionary, but I am an excellent listener and implementer and a good enough administrator.

Although the size and complexity of the Saint Luke's Spiritual Life Center program may seem daunting, their structure has elements that all spiritual life programs could develop. Their committees— Development of the Inner Soul Committee, External Connection Committee, and Infrastructure Committee—suggest three essential elements to consider: inner life development, external relations, and administrative needs.

On a much more modest scale, I was involved with the Committee on Spiritual Nurture at First United Methodist Church in Palo Alto, California, in the late 1980s to early 1990s. For a number of years there had been a Presbyterian mission in the community with an inner life focus. That program offered seasonal retreat days, which had developed a strong ecumenical following. A number of regular participants in these retreat days attended our congregation in Palo Alto. When the purpose of the Presbyterian mission changed, our group wanted to be sure the retreat days would continue.

We created a Committee on Spiritual Nurture for that purpose. Around two hundred people from several different denominations were on our mailing list. Each year our committee planned and implemented four retreat days, one for each season of the year. With the potential for good attendance, we could engage experienced guides from different denominations to lead each retreat day. Most were held at a nearby Franciscan retreat house. Attendance averaged forty to sixty people for a given retreat day. After a few years, the program received a memorial gift of around $1,500. The committee used this fund to draw persons with a national reputation for leadership to an event once a year.

The purpose of the committee was clear, and it aligned with all three themes in the Saint Luke's committee structure: attention to inner life development, external relationships with its focus on ecumenical participation, and infrastructure of hosting these retreat days. In my years of connection with the group, we often thought that we ought to do more within the congregation and occasionally tried new initiatives. They never seemed to last very long. Instead, this single focus—planning and hosting retreat days—seemed to be our mission. It was a rich and enlivening experience for the congregation and for those who served in planning and coordinating the retreat days.

LISTENING TO AND LOVING THE PEOPLE

ROSIE HELMS DESCRIBES her work in spiritual formation development in four mid-sized congregations:

The first church position I held was director of Christian education, responsible for Christian formation for ages two to ninety-two. I came to that position as an experienced educator and growing Christian but had no special training in Christian education beyond my own experience. God had been preparing me for this work in my recently found courage and faith in prayer in my personal life. My own spiritual journey provided strength to step forward into the unknown. I was stepping out of my comfort zone into a zone where I knew prayer would be my tool and God would be my companion. I began the first few days, weeks, and months by praying in my office every day for guidance and direction. A person engaged in ministry must be in a committed relationship with God.

We needed spiritually formed adults to serve in Christian education. Prayer guided my recruitment efforts. I focused on relationships and people who modeled Christian life as a prerequisite for teaching positions. I studied curriculum and sought materials emphasizing formation. One helpful resource was *A Spiritual Formation Workbook*, based on Richard J. Foster's *Streams of Living Water*, in the Renovaré collection. It communicated how we are different in our spiritual preferences and yet all these streams of spirituality are essential to becoming the whole body of Christ.

One outcome of this study was the creation of a ministry to serve the homeless one Saturday a month. The creation of a prayer room was another fruit of the experience. People could come to pray there, come for private worship, and read an array of writings from spiritual writers. There was a place to write intercessory prayer concerns and to record answered prayers. Suggestions for praying for God's realm beyond the church doors were available in the prayer room.

My focus at the next church I served was finding ways to assist the congregation to move from fellowship to formation. At that point I had completed seminary and was consecrated as a probationary deacon. The church already had lots of small groups, but the primary focus was fellowship. I wanted to create a spiritual formation workbook uniquely designed for this congregation. I drew from several resources, including writings of Henri Nouwen and Richard Foster.[4] This resource introduced the reasons we need small groups; it provided an overview of Wesley's class meetings, a theology of discipleship, the role of listening, understanding that faith is not stagnant but formative, and issues of diversity.

I included a brief section on Myers-Briggs personality preferences and patterns of spirituality.

This resource brought people into deeper discussions than they had experienced in the fellowship groups. People were challenged to make connections between their faith and the needs of the world. I made this resource available to the Sunday school teachers and our small groups. Before I left that church, I started a Companions in Christ class. This small-group series is founded on M. Robert Mulholland's definition of spiritual formation: "Spiritual formation is the process of being conformed to the image of Christ by the gracious working of God's spirit, for the transformation of the world." Participating in Companions in Christ groups helps develop the means of grace that move us toward what John Wesley called perfecting love.

Learning together, as brothers and sisters in Christ, and calling one another into accountability were primary arenas of service at Saint Mark's United Methodist in Carmel, Indiana. This is the place where everything I had been learning and working on came to fruition. I was able to work with staff once a week on devotional material and praying together. The pastors prayed together weekly. Here we saw one another not as coworkers but as sisters and brothers in Christ. This congregation, highly educated and motivated, had been excellent in mission work. Learning to share honestly and encourage one another in growing spiritually were growth areas for an otherwise healthy church.

At Saint Mark's I introduced the Companions in Christ series; the church already had strong Disciple Bible Study groups going. I also introduced the labyrinth as another spiritual tool for prayer and formation. (After I left, they installed a labyrinth.) We did a couple of spiritual retreats locally under my leadership and then invited speakers with strengths in spiritual formation to lead retreats at Saint Mark's. Other well-received resources were *Soul Feast* by Marjorie Thompson, *Invitation to a Journey* by M. Robert Mullholland Jr., and the initial draft of Dwight Judy's book *Discerning Life Transitions*. Several people discerned new directions for themselves. Journaling experiences were useful to some people as a means to learn more about themselves and their relationship with God.

First United Methodist Church in Lakeland, Florida, where I now serve, is a truly healthy church growing in spiritual formation. I met people here hungry and willing to encounter a deeper spiritual formation with God. We used Richard Foster's *Celebration of Discipline* at Lent, and the pastors preached on the disciplines. After we provided some training for several small-group leaders, many groups in the congregation delved into Foster's work. We also introduced walking the labyrinth and were able to borrow one to use during Lent.

One thing we learn from Rosie Helms's report is that a gifted leader in spiritual formation can have a major impact within congregations that conceive of their core mission in different ways. Congregations of varying sizes and demographics can all be enriched by attention to inner life development, examining their understanding and approaches to external relationships with sound infrastructure. Rosie concludes by stating what works in shaping these ministry areas: "I found that listening and loving the people is where we begin. Then we are open to God's leading."

PRAYER CONFERENCES FOR CONGREGATION AND COMMUNITY

JANE WATTS WORKED within existing congregational structures to create an emphasis on contemplative prayer. Subsequently, the opportunity arose to develop prayer conferences for the community:

The prayer ministry at my church was well established when my pastor invited me to join a leadership team. We were to implement contemplative offerings for the congregation. The prayer ministry consisted of teams for intercessory prayer, a prayer room where prayer vigils were held on a scheduled basis, and a prayer conference featuring a guest speaker every other year. The semiannual prayer conference alternated with a revival.

Another established pattern at the church was Wednesday-night studies following a meal. So when I began to consider where to open the door to contemplative studies and offerings, this time on Wednesday evenings presented itself. I taught and have continued to teach six-week introductions to contemplative prayer over the years. About the same time these studies were initiated, we also began holding annual three-day silent retreats at a nearby retreat center.

The semiannual prayer conference typically had been fairly didactic, but one year we had an opportunity to invite an out-of-state speaker who taught spiritual prayer practices. Because this teacher belonged to another denomination, we were able to share costs for the presenter with another group in the community. We planned an experiential model for a day retreat, held on a Saturday from 9:30 a.m. until 3:00 p.m. We provided lunch for the participants.

The day began with groups around tables in a large room, where the teacher presented a short history of the spiritual disciplines in the life of the church. We had recruited spiritual directors from the area, practiced in a variety of spiritual disciplines, to guide small groups. Around the large gathering area, rooms were designated for different spiritual disciplines. Participants could choose a discipline that drew their attention and join a small group exploring it with a guide. The guides gave more information about the specific practice they were leading, followed by a time for practicing the discipline itself.

The rhythm of the day permitted each person to try out two spiritual disciplines. There was time for journaling and for sharing in the small groups about the experience of the disciplines. In closing, the outside speaker presented again to the large group. She described models for creating a rule of life, thus inviting the participants to weave practices of prayer into their daily rhythms of meditation and study. We offered a printed bibliography listing various areas of the Christian spiritual life and had a book table with examples of materials for both individual and group contemplative study.

The following year the church decided not to hold a revival, so our team was asked to repeat a prayer conference. Budget constraints meant the event evolved differently, but we again had attendees select two of the experiential sessions in the practice of spiritual disciplines. This time we included not only the classic disciplines but also a few more contemporary practices. Offerings included the arts—writing poetry, praying with mandalas, and movement or body prayer. This prayer conference was held in the evening rather than on a Saturday.

My original inspiration came from Jane Vennard's book *Be Still: Designing and Leading Contemplative Retreats*, which includes guidance in the rhythm of contemplative retreats. She also suggests a model of "home retreat" in settings where people are reluctant to go away on retreat. We do not presently have another prayer conference planned, but multiple Companions in Christ groups are now part of our church life, as well a Stephen Ministry led by trained spiritual directors. My role

has shifted as a way has opened for me to be part of other areas of
ministry planning, weaving spiritual formation practices into the rhythm
of life of my church.

As we have observed before, spiritual formation ministries often
arise from the efforts of inspired individuals who are heeding God's
call to step forward and offer a new vision of Christian life. The Spirit
may blow in different directions. It takes inspired individuals who
are listening for that wind of the Spirit to guide these unfolding possibilities for new life. This new vision involves attention to inner-life
development through the practice of personal disciplines of prayer,
scripture study, and sustained attention to God's inspiration for life
mission and service. We are witnessing a renewal congruent with
similar movements of the inner life in the history of Christianity.
Since the beginning of Christianity, a struggle between the church
as a structure and the inspiration of individuals to follow Christ has
existed. Church history reveals that institutional forms function well
for a while and then deteriorate. New wineskins of one generation
become the old wineskins breaking under the new wine of the Spirit
in another generation. We are living again in such a time.

Denominations are struggling to bring the love of Christ into
forms that match the needs of today's world. Throughout the history
of Christianity, new voices have arisen with a fresh understanding of
the vision of Christ for their time. These individuals typically brought
about renewal by creating a new religious order or a new denomination. The inspired stories gathered in this book suggest an image
linking our present renewal of spiritual life with that historic pattern.
I imagine each of these persons in the role of an abbess or abbot guiding a small community of people who seek a deeper life in Christ.
We witness small communities forming around these individuals
who have steeped themselves in spiritual disciplines. This movement
is reminiscent of the small communities of early seekers that arose
in the desert regions during the first centuries of Christianity. This
movement springs from individuals being called one by one to follow
Jesus in an earnest way. It's all about the power of one person to make
a difference.

DEVELOPING A SPIRITUAL DIRECTION MINISTRY

DIANE STEPHENS, SPIRITUAL director and a ruling elder in the Presbyterian Church (USA), describes the challenges of living into such a ministry calling. She has had an impact on both local congregations and the ethos of her denomination:

An ordained ruling elder in the Presbyterian Church (USA), I was called to ministry in the mid-1990s but not to parish ministry. I loved the study of Christian spirituality and the practice of spiritual formation! It took awhile to find a seminary degree program that met both my academic and formational needs, to close my communication business, and then to offer spiritual formation full-time. I completed my master's program in 2001.

When I was launching a ministry of spiritual formation in 2001, I started with retreats. It felt like a natural place to begin. I wanted to remain self-employed and move into ministry by building on strengths and skills developed while running my own marketing communication business for almost twenty years. Keynote presentations, workshops, and seminars were familiar, exciting ways to engage people and topics I care about.

Within a few months, I had scheduled events with several Presbyterian, United Methodist, American Baptist, and United Church of Christ congregations. Beginning a retreat ministry was the easy part. Sustaining and growing it has been something else. After that first wave of interest in retreats, some congregations expressed interest in sponsoring weekend getaways but wanted to check me out first. Leading adult education programs on Sunday mornings, weeknights, or during Lent has allowed congregations to sample my leadership style as well as program content; ongoing, repeated contact has advanced long-term connections. In addition to teaching in congregations, I am an affiliate faculty in spiritual formation at Garrett-Evangelical Theological Seminary, and I serve as faculty on the Presbyterian CREDO program of renewal, an eight-day conference-retreat for PCUSA pastors.

A couple of years into ministry, I noticed that my energy peaked when talking one-on-one with retreat and class participants, and they began to ask me about spiritual direction. Was I taking new directees? Their interest was a wake-up call to begin offering spiritual direction.

I joined a peer supervision group and contacted the pastor of First Congregational Church of Wilmette, Illinois, to ask whether the church might host a ministry of spiritual direction. We worked out an arrangement whereby I preach once a year in exchange for office space on Mondays and Thursdays. I also provide congregational retreats on a reduced-fee basis and ensure that members of the congregation have priority in scheduling spiritual direction. Since I am certified to administer and interpret the Myers-Briggs Type Indicator, the pastor refers engaged couples to me for premarital counseling. I am listed as spiritual director in residence in the congregation's communication.

The biggest challenge of this self-supporting ministry is income. While what I do is life-giving, the income it produces is barely enough to eke out a living. Two other challenges: staying on top of economic and other trends and exploring additional delivery models, such as online courses, podcasts, and blogging.

What sustains me are the people I meet, and how earnest they are about their spiritual journeys. I have also come to count on my advisory board and Presbyterian spiritual directors group for wisdom, program ideas, varied denominational viewpoints, contacts, and referrals as well as their interest and support. I cannot imagine the shape or quality of my ministry without the love and encouragement of my covenant group. The four of us—two United Methodist pastors, one United Church of Christ pastor, and one Presbyterian elder—have been together since 1993. Continuing education renews me, as does membership in such professional organizations as Spiritual Directors International, Society for the Study of Christian Spirituality, and North American Academy of Liturgy. Programming, research, writing, and networking all feed my soul and my ministry.

Diane Stephens describes both the rewards and the difficulties of creating an independent spiritual formation ministry. Many people are being called into this pioneering work. Spiritual life centers, such as the ones described in this chapter, often offer spiritual direction. Could more churches incorporate spiritual direction as part of spiritual life ministries?

Shelagh Donoghue described the conversion of a space for shared practice of spiritual direction at Saint Francis Xavier Roman Catholic Church, also in Wilmette, Illinois. Several trained laypersons, in addition to two parish staff members, provide spiritual direction at the parish. Two small rooms have been designated for this purpose and furnished comfortably.

The facility now houses parish administrative offices, a chapel with flexible seating so it can also function as a meeting room, a comfortable gathering room, and a small kitchen to provide hospitality. When I inquired about how the space is reserved for spiritual direction, Shelagh opened a closet door and showed me a calendar. It's as simple as people noting on the calendar the times that they would like to use the room. About six spiritual directors—not all Saint Francis Xavier parishioners—share the space. Many congregations could create a small prayer room that could be reserved from time to time for individual and small-group spiritual direction.

◆ ◆ ◆

Diana Butler Bass offered a surprising analysis of contemporary American Christianity in *Christianity for the Rest of Us: How the Neighborhood Church Is Transforming the Faith*. The hope she expresses echoes throughout these pages as congregations find vitality through a spiritual life focus:

> Many people think mainline Protestantism is dying, that it is going the way of the dodo in favor of a more lively form of conservative Christianity found in suburban evangelical megachurches. I do not deny that mainline Protestantism is in trouble. Some of its institutions, unresponsive to change, are probably beyond hope of recovery or repair. I also believe, however, that lively faith is not located in buildings, programs, organizations, and structures. Rather, spiritual vitality lives in human beings; it is located in the heart of God's people and the communities they form. At the edges of mainline institutional decay, some remarkable congregations are finding new ways of being faithful—ways that offer hope to those Americans who want to be Christian but are wary of the religion found in those suburban megachurches.[5]

Christianity after Religion: The End of Church and the Birth of a New Spiritual Awakening, also by Bass, paints a more pessimistic picture of the church's future.[6] But the stories in *A Quiet Pentecost* witness to a new spiritual awakening occurring within mainline congregations. These are examples of congregations that have learned how to "invite the Spirit." While it has become popular to decry the vitality of the church, we are witnessing not the death of the church but its rebirth through a quiet Pentecost among us.

Congregations are being led into spiritual vitality in new ways, often naming spiritual formation ministries as a unique focus in their life together. Vision means more than the size of a congregation. As we have seen, individuals are praying for inspiration and receiving vision for this kind of ministry. The spiritual formation movement, which began in earnest in the 1980s in Protestant Christianity, is now maturing with resources for small-group study, educational programs, and models to which we can point for guidance. As leaders in spiritual formation, you and your spiritual life team are invited by the Holy Spirit to dream how to reveal the treasures of Christian spiritual life to one another and to your communities. You are leaven in the bread of Jesus Christ. Begin small or large, but begin!

CHAPTER SEVEN

Inviting the Spirit:
A NOT-SO-QUIET PENTECOST

The wind blows where it chooses,
and you hear the sound of it,
but you do not know where it comes from or where it goes.
So it is with everyone who is born of the Spirit.
—John 3:8

WHEN JOHN THE Baptist sent word to Jesus asking, "Are you the one who is to come or are we to wait for another?" Jesus answered, "Go and tell John what you hear and see: the blind receive their sight, the lame walk, the lepers are cleansed, the deaf hear, the dead are raised, and the poor have good news brought to them. And blessed is anyone who takes no offense at me" (Matt. 11:3-6). Jesus is saying, "Look at what is happening." While contributors to this collection of stories do not claim such miraculous healings, their accounts do show us spiritual formation practices that work. They show us what happens when people open themselves to the Holy Spirit. Look and see. People are finding their lives enriched with prayer practices. They are enlivening their congregations with art and pauses from a world gone mad with frenzied activity. They are discovering their own summons to ministry through prayer and disciplined study of scripture. They are discerning mission for their communities. Is this a Pentecost for our times? Come and see!

In describing radical hospitality, Robert Schnase asks, "How do people hear about your church? In what ways are members encouraged to invite and welcome people? How are laity prepared for the work of invitation and hospitality?"[1] People are finding the power of prayer inspires new forms of welcome. Some congregations practice a "longest night" service of healing prayer, with particular outreach to persons suffering physical illnesses. They become known in their communities as the place where healing prayers and anointing are regularly offered. Congregations in the same community may rotate responsibility for a Taizé service on a monthly basis, so that a weekly Taizé experience is available. LifeHouse Ministries issues an invitation for a shared meal with people in their neighborhood every two weeks. TheLifewell Free Store was birthed into existence through prayer in Zanesville, Ohio. A study of *A Spiritual Formation Workbook* in another congregation inspired both outreach in service to the homeless and in-reach through the creation of a prayer room. The false dichotomy of inner life and outward mission dissolves when people take their life of faith seriously.

PRAYER FOR THE WORLD

ROSIE HELMS DESCRIBES a prayer ministry outreach to the community beyond the church walls in Lakeland, Florida:

Our church completed a huge mission in the area around our church. The mission "Celebrate Jesus" was conceived and is being practiced in Florida.[2] It takes a lot of work and incorporates a lot of people working together in mission. Several leaders work on the event months in advance. I served as the prayer coordinator.

Our team went door-to-door leaving an invitation to our block party and a prayer plant for each neighbor. We asked people if we could pray for them about any concerns they had. Each group, including youth and adults, had one person who had already participated in a similar mission week. We all wore yellow shirts printed with "Celebrate Jesus." We were very recognizable. We asked for nothing! We wanted to show our neighbors that we are a church that cares, and we care because God cares.

Everybody found out how much need there was around us and that they could pray for people on the spot, making a difference in their lives. A lot of people came to the block party. It was a huge success, mainly because it was bathed in prayer for months ahead of time. People really had a chance to see God at work that week. The book *Why Pray?* was an excellent resource for helping people see the power of prayer and the difference it makes for families to pray together to live out Jesus' mission to make disciples.

Many ideas came out of this week about ways to continue serving our neighbors. As a result, our prayer shawl ministry is now well organized and has shawls ready for future requests. We will see the fruit of this mission for a long time to come. It was transformational not only for the neighborhood but also for our congregation. Listening and loving the people is where we begin. Then we are open to God's leading. We start where individuals are spiritually and pray with them for a deeper, wider journey with God.

A dramatic renewal of life and mission is happening in the African Methodist Episcopal Church South District in Chicago at Fifth Sunday gatherings of the whole district. Sheila Wilson-Freelon's enthusiasm is contagious as she relates the Fifth Sunday Story: Fueling Flames of Holy Ghost Power:

Today, in my role as a district director of evangelism, I lead a thriving transformative ministry in the Sizzling South District of the Chicago Conference of the Fourth Episcopal District of the African Methodist Episcopal Church. Four times a year, hundreds of people participate in a mini Fire-Filled Revival and Evangelistic Crusade under the ministry's theme: Love, Unity, One Accord=Holy Ghost Power. Our theme for the worship services is Come Feel the Fire: Fueling Flames of Holy Ghost Power.

This ministry brings nineteen churches together each Fifth Sunday at a designated church in the South District. The contemporary services are upbeat with a charismatic move of the Holy Spirit. For each service, we wear unity colors, which have either spiritual or cultural significance (i.e., white for purity of the Holy Spirit or Afrocentric attire for Black History Month). The ministry serves to strengthen four areas of our spiritual lives in Christ Jesus: (1) love of Christ, love of neighbor, unity and one accord; (2) kingdom building; (3) Christian fellowship; (4) deeper prayer life. The most important of these emphases is promoting the Love of Christ, Love of Neighbor, Unity and One Accord among the nineteen churches, as found in Acts 2.

In 2008 Presiding Elder Thomas M. Hughes gave me the opportunity to develop a vision for inspiring nineteen churches to: (1) love and support each other and (2) develop a love for building the kingdom of God together. In response to my prayers, God gave me a multifaceted vision and mission through scripture to bring the bride of Christ together in praise, worship, teaching, and fellowship, with the ultimate goal being kingdom building. The specific text that inspired all of this is Acts 2:42-47.

During worship, each host pastor delivers a sermon on our theme. This service is a catalyst for the ongoing nurture of the four attributes described above long after the Fifth Sunday worship service has ended. Additionally, the presiding elder and I (as worship leader) promote and encourage Acts 2—Love of Christ, Love of Neighbor, Unity and One Accord—as we address the congregation. The Saturday before the Sunday worship, the district evangelism team provides Friendship and Street Evangelism training to the host church members. Through these kingdom-building efforts, the ministry trains churches to win souls for Christ as they canvas the neighborhoods by distributing flyers and inviting residents to the Fifth Sunday worship and fellowship.

To support a deeper prayer life among district members, our presiding elder had previously established a district prayer team and required each local church to establish a prayer team for evangelistic purposes. The district prayer and evangelism teams pray in and anoint the host church with blessed oil the Saturday before the worship service. On the day of the worship service, we pray for love, unity, one accord, blessings, salvation, and protection for an entire hour before the service begins. Prayers for the manifestation of the Holy Spirit and for the anointing of all in attendance also go forth. This Holy Spirit anointing equips us with spiritual power to effectively minister in preaching, teaching, giving, and evangelism for the glory of God.

Participants have expressed their enjoyment of the worship and the fellowship. Many have informed me that they feel the fire of the Holy Spirit in these meetings. Those who have canvassed and invited the neighborhood initially expressed apprehension about participating in street evangelism; however, they return from these activities reporting stories of praying with and leading people to Christ on the streets in the Chicagoland area. They return from their street evangelism activities floating on a spiritual cloud as the Holy Spirit anointed them with the joy of witnessing. As a result, more and more churches are engaging in street evangelism. More significantly, more souls are being saved and given access to fundamental gospel truths. The spiritual life force in the district is very positive as the Holy Spirit honors our efforts to model the dedication of the church in Acts 2. As a direct result of this ministry, a new church has been started in the district. Another has changed its name to Unity Temple. Both initiatives were approved by Presiding Elder Hughes and Bishop John R. Bryant, Senior Bishop and Presiding Prelate of the AME Church.

I am humbled by my God-given vision, God's vision in action, and the impact the Holy Spirit is making in the life of the AME Church. I recognize that I could not have done this without (1) the Holy Spirit and (2) the tremendous support given to me by our Presiding Elder Hughes and the Sizzling South District churches. We give God all the glory, honor, and praise for Fueling the Flames of His Holy Ghost Power in evangelistic revival throughout our unifying district and the community. To God we are forever grateful.

This ministry focus embodies the three elements we discovered in the committee structure at Saint Luke's UMC: inner life development, external relations, and administrative needs. This collective gathering of Christians in the name of Christ emboldens them to take their love and generosity into the streets surrounding their congregations.

RENEWING INTERCESSORY PRAYER TEAMS

MOST CHURCHES HAVE some form of intercessory prayer group or prayer team. Such groups may pray regularly with worship leaders before worship. Usually they are available as a telephone tree for emergency concerns within the congregation. Sometimes they meet face-to-face to pray weekly for concerns that have surfaced within the congregation. With electronic technology now available, prayer requests may be circulated via e-mail. If a prayer team is already meeting regularly, it could become a model small group for prayer and spiritual nurture within the congregation. New ministry emphases might arise if these committed people think and pray together about the mission of the congregation.

A very effective prayer team model was created in the mid-1990s by Anita Fenstermacher (now deceased). In this model, prayer team participants are invited to indicate how long they can commit to the prayer ministry—three months, six months, one year, indefinitely. They covenant to pray for any request immediately upon hearing about it, as well as to contact the next designated person on the telephone tree or to keep calling down the list until reaching the next person. They commit to quarterly gatherings for instruction on prayer and mutual enrichment. They were honored in this ministry with an annual commissioning in a worship service. Those who request prayer are asked how long they wish to be kept on the prayer list and whether they want their request to remain anonymous or not. Finally, the team follows up each week with people who requested prayer. This structure provides a good way to track concerns for pastoral care within the congregation as well as to keep prayer requests current.

A daily devotional format incorporating prayer requests is another model for intercessory prayer. Devotions and current prayer requests are sent out to prayer team members weekly. A simple and meaningful version of this devotional approach takes the form of Morning Prayer, a historic prayer of the church, as the opening; adds daily lectionary scripture readings for the week; lists the various categories of prayer requests; and concludes with the Lord's Prayer.

Along with using a resource such as this, the prayer team might learn a *lectio divina* prayer practice to steep their intercessory prayers in the scripture text for the day. Just as there are many ways to pray, there can be many ways to frame intercessions. People may find Centering Prayer, for example, a particularly meaningful way to pray for others. After centering in God's loving presence, specific prayer needs can be brought to mind, often without words, but simply to be bathed in God's grace.

DEFINING SPIRITUALITY IN YOUR CONGREGATION

THESE REFLECTIONS ON prayer teams and intercessory prayer suggest that the church has an opportunity to renew its life of prayer and spiritual formation in creative ways. Numerous resources could be used for a congregational study. One useful approach to defining spirituality comes from a book by Ernest Boyer Jr., *A Way in the World: Family Life as Spiritual Discipline.* Boyer uses the images of the "spirituality of the center" and "spirituality of the edge." These two images convey key issues for us to consider as we reflect on the spiritual life of our congregation and community. By *spirituality of the center,* Boyer means our life in family relationships and our life in the world. *Spirituality of the edge* refers to taking time apart, away from our daily life and concerns. When considering a congregation's ministry of spiritual formation, are both of these dimensions addressed?

For example, in the realm of spirituality of the center, are there support groups for various life concerns—for parents of young children, for caregivers of persons with health challenges, and so forth? Spirituality of the edge programs might teach spiritual disciplines that enable people to pause in the midst of daily life and renew themselves in the presence of God. People need to recall God's promise of redemptive renewal regularly.

A number of resources can provide a framework for thinking about prayer and spiritual formation within the congregation. One of the best is Marjorie Thompson's *Soul Feast*. Reading *Soul Feast* together as a spiritual life team can assist you in determining spiritual disciplines your congregation may wish to foster. The book works through personal and corporate disciplines, including prayer, worship, hospitality, and spiritual direction; it also contains a study guide for group conversation.

Studying Patricia Brown's *Paths to Prayer* is another good way to start or continue conversation about various types of prayer within your spiritual formation team and your congregation. Brown describes forty prayer forms, clustered into four categories: searching prayer, experiential prayer, relational prayer, and innovative prayer. She provides an inventory to determine personal preferences.

In a classic approach, *Prayer and Temperament: Different Prayer Forms for Different Personality Types* by Michael and Norrisey uses Roman Catholic figures and historical references along with Myers-Briggs personality typology to explore prayer. The authors describe prayer forms in terms of Benedictine, Augustinian, Franciscan, and Thomistic tendencies. *A Spiritual Formation Workbook: Small-Group Resources for Nurturing Christian Growth* by Smith and Graybeal works through six primary forms of Christian spirituality as described by Richard J. Foster in *Streams of Living Water*: contemplative, holiness, charismatic, social justice, evangelical, and incarnational. It provides a way to learn about these rich streams in Christian history and how to apply them today.

Jane Watts names the key elements, including books and resource persons, for developing a long-term curriculum in spiritual formation:

> The categories of resources I have found vital in these introductory settings for local congregations include: (1) books regarding history grounded in the mainstream Christian tradition of the church; (2) books with models of introductions to classic spiritual disciplines; (3) books with examples of classic disciplines as well as contemporary adaptations of practices of prayer grounded in the classic disciplines; (4) people to offer leadership. There may be people in your region with whom you can connect to broaden the leadership for small groups, retreats, or prayer conferences. For additional persons who are trained in spiritual direction or spiritual formation leadership, look to Hearts on Fire: Fellowship of United Methodist Spiritual Directors and Retreat Leaders or Spiritual Directors International for persons in your region.[3] Other resources may be available through local Episcopal and Catholic dioceses or Christian retreat centers or monasteries. Presbyterian (PCUSA) and Lutheran (ELCA) churches may provide resources nationally and regionally.

Jane Watts models what can happen for any who initiate a spiritual formation emphasis: "I don't lead all of the offerings at my church. I now organize them and invite and connect and lean upon the growing community of soul friends traveling this common journey and sharing their gifts in guiding others along the way."

CHALLENGES TO A QUIET PENTECOST

BARBARA HALE, ACTIVE in spiritual formation work regionally and in congregations in two different states, notes the continuing difficulties in sustaining a spiritual formation focus. When leaders or committee structures change, well-established programs may suffer. The pioneering nature of spiritual formation ministries is underscored by an encounter she had with a seminary professor. "When I said I'd been in spiritual direction for ten years, he said, 'What's wrong?'" Of course, those of us in spiritual direction ministries think of spiritual direction as a lifelong process that all pastors should undertake. "When I worked in business," Barbara comments, "I learned that if you don't have support at the top, it's difficult to get programs started and for them to have continued support. I'm sure you can generalize this idea to churches." Many of the contributors to this book have alluded to this difficulty.

Barbara also notes the difference between more recently ordained pastors and those who received their seminary education before seminaries increased curriculum offerings in prayer and spiritual disciplines. "With the lack of education in spiritual disciplines and acquaintance with the ancient mystics, ministers do not have knowledge of the different facets of spiritual formation unless they have had a personal interest in this work." The thesis of this book is that spiritual formation as a discipline for seminary and church is here to stay. But, since it is a newer field in the seminary curriculum, clergy currently serving churches may not have been taught about this rich stream of Christian tradition. Funding for continuing education for clergy may or may not be focused in spiritual formation areas.

Mary Hooper recorded the challenge in sustaining a Centering Prayer group and also remarked on the need for further education of church leaders: "The training of spiritual leaders needs to include training in spiritual formation and contemplative practices. Until church leadership recognizes the need for contemplative practices within the church, many will seek spiritual experiences from outside their religious traditions." To this plea Cherri Johnson adds an important element: "It is essential that we, as the church, raise up more clergy and laity steeped in the practice of spiritual formation—accountable to their faith journey, with communities in which they can face their own shadow and do their deeper inner work."

Contemplative prayer inevitably leads us into a hard look at our own psychological weaknesses and fractured relationships. For this reason many people resist the call to inner work. But without this inner work, church leaders will continue to falter. With disciplined personal prayer life and accountability, the church of the future can be renewed in creative ways. Cherri Johnson continues, "I believe this is the call placed on the emerging church—not simply addressing programmatic concerns but raising up and empowering spiritual leadership—clergy and laity committed to the deeper journey, leading others toward authentic transformation. This in turn will transform the world in which we live."

Pastors and other church leaders can be encouraged to find a spiritual director or a group for spiritual support. Janis Blean-Kachigan has worked with a group of seven women pastors from three denominations over a period of eight years. They have engaged in the deep inner work necessary for sustaining spiritual leadership:

> For the first couple of years the group met monthly for ninety minutes. Each time, I offered different spiritual disciplines. We explored *lectio divina*, body prayer, chanting, Centering Prayer, and questions for reflection. There was always sharing, which was invited from participants' professional as well as personal lives. Often we would conclude with a time of prayer—sometimes for each individual, sometimes the intercessions of our hearts. We frequently met at the denominational headquarters of a couple of the participants.
>
> In the third year, changes in our format were necessary for several reasons. We shifted from a ninety-minute gathering each month to a quarterly daylong retreat held at a retreat center. We have continued to use the same kind of spiritual formation disciplines during our days of retreat, and since we have moved to the retreat model, I have placed much more emphasis on process—on how we are with one another. I have drawn heavily upon the work of Parker Palmer, specifically *A Hidden Wholeness: Journey Toward an Undivided Life*, and his DVD *Circles of Trust*. Through the slow, steady exploration and application of these principles, the group has developed a tender, safe sense of intimacy, which fosters ever-unfolding spiritual and emotional maturity.
>
> What benefits do the participants experience? Support for the journey, an increased awareness of the Holy One, genuine spiritual companionship and friendship, increased spiritual and emotional maturity, an ever-increasing ability to enter into challenge and vulnerability, a gentle softening of the self. My observation is that there is great benefit in the peer-group direction process, as participants learn, grow, and at times are profoundly touched via another's journey and process.

Such groups of spiritual discipline and support make a profound difference in the viability of ministers and for all Christians. We are made for community, and we are made for service.

As I have compiled this book, I have been greatly encouraged that the Holy Spirit is alive in the hearts of individuals and congregations as we learn to listen and respond to divine nudges. I have been reminded of the witness of Church of the Saviour, started in the mid-1940s by Gordon and Mary Cosby. The vitality of this unique church has been in attending to both the journey inward and the journey outward. The need today is as great as it has ever been to create church structures that allow for genuine creativity to emerge. A gift we can all receive from their model of ministry is to nourish the call of the individual to mission. In the Church of the Saviour, if a person receives an idea for mission in the name of Christ, it is announced at a community gathering. If one other person shares the same vision, they get to work, dreaming how such a mission of service might be developed. Many different forms of ministry groups emerged under this model. Elizabeth O'Connor provided invaluable insights to the Church of the Saviour through her understanding of the inner life and its manifestation in outward service. Her writings chronicled this significant church renewal movement in the twentieth century. She writes about the importance of continually listening inwardly for God's calling to the individual heart. The pioneers of spiritual formation ministries are giving themselves unreservedly to the truth of spiritual life for these times. They are showing us the way into a meaningful life with God through prayer and service.

Elizabeth O'Connor's words to the church of the twentieth century are equally valid in the twenty-first century:

> We can discover the twentieth-century structures, learn modern techniques, and originate challenging programs, but these in themselves are not enough. They may win people to our organizations, but not to the living Christ. For this we need men and women abandoned to God, contagiously radiant because in their inner lives a conversation goes on with Him who is Lord. They are the people who fill one's soul with a free, spontaneous worship. Thoughts begin to hurdle the usual boundaries, and you wonder why you ever doubted. In their presence your spirit has wings; you sense the very presence of God.[4]

I hope you have found such persons in this book. Today we need to abandon ourselves to God, to listen for inspiration, to gather companions for prayerful support, and to act. We must link again *opus dei, opus manuum,* and *lectio divina* in regular practices of *hospitality* within each of our communities, in the name of Christ.

ALLOWING JESUS TO LEAD US

THE STORIES COLLECTED here are meant to ignite images of new life through prayer—in your heart and in your congregation. John Anderson tells how one congregation has been profoundly transformed by learning to listen together for divine guidance throughout the life of the congregation:

> After completing the first year of Companions in Christ curriculum at Trinity Presbyterian Church in Arvada, Colorado, we decided to experiment with practicing discernment as a session [the elder board of a Presbyterian church]. And it was indeed an experiment. We gathered on a weekend retreat, identified two issues to discern together, and then mechanically followed the steps outlined in *Discerning God's Will Together: A Spiritual Practice for the Church* by Charles Olsen and Danny Morris. We did not fully understand what we were doing. We just hoped that Jesus would lead our conversation and that we'd know how to recognize it when he did. The elders of our church were stunned by the results. In both issues, we discovered Jesus leading us to conclusions that none of us could have predicted ahead of time. That was twelve years ago, and we've been hooked on asking Jesus to guide us ever since!
>
> A few years later I attended a conference titled "Discerning the Leadership of Christ." During a panel discussion at that event, Gordon Smith (author of *The Voice of Jesus: Discernment, Prayer and the Witness of the Spirit*) posited the idea that "Jesus wants to lead his church in *real time.*" He asserted that Jesus has a unique will for each church and that he yearns to guide every congregation toward his purpose for them. Until that point, I had always assumed that Christ led his church through principles and precepts revealed in scripture. It never occurred to me that Jesus might have a more specific will for my congregation, a will that could be discovered only through recognizing his present leadership. So we committed ourselves to a deeper exploration of discerning the guidance of Jesus together.
>
> We found the initial process of group discernment outlined by Olsen and Morris to be too cumbersome for us. So we began to define a

simpler methodology for how we could listen for the voice of Jesus guiding our church. In the end, following specific steps in the discernment process was not as important as a few key spiritual practices of discernment: (1) sharing our insights and listening for the witness of the Spirit in what was offered; (2) reflecting on how our predispositions to certain outcomes might prevent us from hearing God's will; (3) meditating on scripture together as a means for the Spirit to reveal a way forward; and (4) continuing to listen even as we implemented the outcome of our discernment.

In the first several years of practicing discernment, we mistakenly believed that the goal of discernment was to arrive at a God-directed decision. However, we discovered that God was more concerned about our formation than our conclusions. Jesus often led us by stages, and we learned to honor that. He seemed to prefer to reveal his purposes one stepping stone at a time, while we preferred to see the whole path stretched out before us. Learning to become comfortable with not knowing what was next became an important transition in our leadership team.

Our elders began to see group discernment as a rich spiritual practice. As we identified God speaking to us in scripture and sensed the Spirit guiding our insights, many elders experienced God personally addressing them! It was exhilarating to recognize God leading our church. We found the courage to follow wherever we believed God was guiding us.

One of our first clues that practicing discernment involved more than making decisions was the amount of personal change required to affirm God's will. Whenever we dealt with a highly charged issue, no one in the room was left unchanged by the solution Jesus placed before us. In other words, everyone found that Christ was asking them to change in some way to be able to affirm the conclusion that he desired. It became clear that reaching a decision together was secondary to the spiritual formation of our leadership team.

The session once made a big decision that involved changing the style of worship for our church. As leaders, we felt convinced that God was guiding us. However, we discovered that it was not enough for the elders to discern God's will on behalf of the church. They may also need to guide the entire congregation in recognizing God's will together. The session found themselves in a new role: listening for the voice of Jesus alongside the congregation rather than for them. In the end, our church came to a different conclusion together than our leaders had on their own. And six weeks of congregational discernment exercises allowed the whole church family to learn how to better recognize the leadership of Jesus in their lives as well.

More than a process for making decisions together, group discernment has become a primary means for following Jesus in our daily lives.

If the church of our time is to come to the shared spirit of love described in the early church, we must learn new ways to be together in the Spirit and new ways to listen together in Christ for divine guidance. The old ways of making decisions based on the best of our human understanding, debating alternatives, and struggling over outcomes is not enough. Again and again in these pages we have witnessed an alternate way. John Anderson tells of a whole congregation basing its decision processes on this way. The seeming "nothing" of prayerful silence is given form in ways to enable a congregation to listen together for guidance from the resurrected Christ. But notice the patience that is required. In this example, even the church council's decision was allowed to seep into the life of the whole congregation and to be changed in the process.

Life in Christ does not allow for complacency. In the introduction I quoted Thomas Merton describing the risk involved in every act of prayer. Now we see that the risk extends to our faith communities as well. When we take seriously the calling to immerse all decisions within the "paschal rhythm," to submit all life within the church to the principles of the Crucifixion-Resurrection cycle of renewal, we are in unknown territory. Yet, what are we here for if not to learn to participate again and again in the new life offered by such transcendent hope? Merton's words are worth repeating:

> There is a "movement" of meditation, expressing the basic "paschal" rhythm of the Christian life, the passage from death to life in Christ. Sometimes prayer, meditation and contemplation are "death"—a kind of descent into our own nothingness, a recognition of helplessness, frustration, infidelity, confusion, ignorance. Note how common this theme is in the Psalms. . . . Then as we determine to face the hard realities of our inner life, as we

recognize once again that we need to pray hard and humbly for faith, [God] draws us out of darkness into light—grants us the help we require—if only by giving us more faith to believe that [God] can and will help us in [God's] own time. This is already a sufficient answer.[5]

CHAPTER EIGHT

Inviting the Spirit into
YOUR FAITH COMMUNITY

A Guide for Starting or Strengthing a
Spiritual Formation Ministry

THE HOLY SPIRIT is ready to guide your congregation into a quiet Pentecost. The Spirit's guidance will be quite specific for your congregation and your community. There is no cookie-cutter pattern to enhance your spiritual life or move toward developing a spiritual life center for your congregation and community. Instead, Jesus wants to lead you into unique patterns of prayer, small-group support, local and global mission, and sustaining worship.

Each chapter of this book can be a springboard for conversation among the lay and pastoral leadership of your congregation. Start with the first step in "Getting Started" below—designing a team to work through this book together on behalf of your congregation. Use the questions related to each chapter as a guide for your group's conversation in a series of meetings.

SUGGESTED PATTERN FOR GROUP MEETINGS

FOR EACH MEETING, provide a simple focal point in your gathering place, perhaps a candle, cross, or other symbolic image. After people have gathered, sit together and read the scripture at the beginning of the section you will be discussing. Do a brief personal check in; then share reflections on the reading. Invite people to discuss each question. Everyone doesn't have to comment on every question. Some people will have thoughts related to a particular question or theme; others will be inspired by another question.

Invite all participants to read the questions at home before they read the related chapter. Read the book in the spirit of *lectio divina*, lingering over particular passages, stories, or images that strike you as significant for your congregation. It is helpful for group members to keep a journal of reflections as they read.

Invite prayer partners for the period in between your sessions. Look over questions for the *next* section you will read together. As you close, center yourselves in prayer. As your group becomes more comfortable with the tasks of this work, experiment with different prayer forms or ways of responding as a group to one another's visions for your spiritual life ministry.

After studying the book, you may decide to share particular chapters with certain groups in your congregation. For example, your evangelism work area might look at chapter 7 for ideas on how to increase visibility of your congregation within the community. Your administrative body, missions, and social outreach committees might study chapter 3. Let the Spirit guide you in sharing this resource with your whole congregation. Recall Jesus' words: "I am the vine, you are the branches. . . . My Father is glorified by this, that you bear much fruit and become my disciples" (John 15:5, 8).

GETTING STARTED

1. *Forming a team.* If you do not already have a spiritual life or spiritual formation committee in your congregation, work with your pastor and administrative body to develop a task force to work for six months or more in prayerfully considering potential new areas of ministry. You may want to use an existing prayer ministry group such as an intercessory prayer team.

2. *Covenanting together.* This work will require commitment and prayer. Set a regular time to meet. Commit to regular prayer for the work of this task force or committee. Be committed both to inspiration arising from prayer and to practical tasks of information gathering.

3. At your first meeting explore the two themes below. There are no right answers to these two questions—only what is right for your congregation!

a. *What is your definition of spirituality?* What is the range of subject matter that will be effective in your congregation? Be realistic! Do not push edges too quickly. Think about what people need within your own setting and what kinds of resources will be well received.

b. *Is your work for your congregation only or is it for the broader community as well?* What are implications of promoting your classes, groups, retreats, and so on to those beyond your congregation?

Keep these notes. You'll return to these themes.

4. Review what you are doing in prayer ministries and spiritual formation. For instance, do you have a prayer team ministry? ministries of distribution of Holy Communion to the home bound? Do administrative meetings incorporate a spirit of prayer? How are children and youth ministries formed in prayer and use of scripture for faith formation?

5. Investigate what other congregations in your community are doing in the arena of spiritual formation. What retreat centers are within a drive of one to three hours? How could you research programs, retreat centers, and spiritual directors who might help resource your work? Divide these tasks among your group.

6. Set your next meeting time. State your prayer covenant clearly for this work before the next meeting and close with prayer.

CHAPTER 1: INVITING THE SPIRIT INTO SMALL GROUPS

1. In what ways has your definition of spirituality changed after reading this chapter?
2. Discuss your group's experience with practices like *lectio divina*, Companions in Christ, covenant groups, faith sharing. What type of groups might work well in your congregation?
3. Who might serve as small-group leaders? Who might make brief presentations on spiritual disciplines to your administrative body?

4. What difficulties do you anticipate in developing a spiritual formation focus? Think about using communication tools (newsletter, website, worship bulletin) to describe various types of small groups to your congregation.

CHAPTER 2: INVITING THE SPIRIT INTO WORSHIP

1. In what ways does your group think worship leads to peace both within the community and in all relationships? How might your worship experiences be enhanced in this respect?
2. Discuss the worship experiences currently offered in your congregation. Is there a need for some new worship experience, like Evening Prayer, healing prayer, or Taizé? Should worship be offered at alternate times? Do you have an active worship planning team in your congregation? If so, how could the spiritual formation planning group interface with the worship team?
3. What opportunities are there for "sensory-rich" worship? Consider how your congregation observes the different seasons of the church year. How might your worship space be enhanced with attention to symbolic and artistic expression during these seasons?
4. Consider organizing a churchwide school of prayer.
5. What groups are a regular part of worship? How might teaching prayer disciplines to those groups enhance the worship experience of the entire congregation? Sharing *lectio divina* with such groups is one possibility.

CHAPTER 3: INVITING THE SPIRIT INTO MISSION DISCERNMENT

1. List the ministries of mission, outreach, and service in which your congregation engages. Which ones are still thriving? Which ones need an infusion of new energy?
2. How does your congregation link prayer and service? Can these two dimensions of congregational life be linked more intentionally? Be open to new ideas for making this linkage more vital.

3. How do new areas of mission and service arise in your congregation? How free are individuals to offer ideas? How do these work through governing structures to become named ministries?

4. How are larger needs of the community identified? What new opportunities are possible within your community?

5. Is it time for a planning circle or a planning retreat to think creatively about where God is calling your congregation to mission and service?

6. What simple acts of appreciation and hospitality might your spiritual formation team begin, such as notes of appreciation to persons engaged in clear areas of service?

CHAPTER 4: INVITING THE SPIRIT INTO AGE-LEVEL MINISTRIES

1. What preconceptions about both young and elder adults have been challenged in this chapter? Which examples give you ideas for your congregation? Consider a 24/7 prayer vigil for your whole congregation.

2. Are there opportunities for interfaith experiences within your congregation and community? Is it appropriate in your setting to foster conversation around this topic?

3. The Interfaith Council at Sedgebrook functions as "ambassadors of community peace and goodwill." Invite different groups within your congregations to be such ambassadors on a rotating basis. Each group will define what being "ambassadors of community peace and goodwill" means in your congregation for one or two months; then pass the function to another group.

4. What role might art play in the spiritual formation of your congregation? Think about telling the story of faith visually. Consider inviting artists in the congregation—or the youth under guidance—to create murals or other visual expressions.

5. How might your congregation add a physical health and wellness component to its spiritual formation ministry?

CHAPTER 5: INVITING THE SPIRIT INTO PRAYER
GROUPS

1. What surprised you and your team members in reading these examples of prayer and spiritual formation? What intrigued you?
2. Revisit your own working definition of spirituality and spiritual formation as applicable in your congregation and your community. What changes, if any, would you make?
3. Are there resources nearby for walking the prayer labyrinth? Use the online labyrinth locator at *http://labyrinthlocator.com/*. Take a group on an excursion to experience the labyrinth as prayer. Visit *www.veriditas.org* for more information on the use of the prayer labyrinth.
4. What small groups for women already exist? Might they be interested in developing a spiritual formation focus? What about groups for men? Ask if men over fifty, for example, would like to form a meditation and spiritual formation group.
5. Your team might select one book as a resource to begin studying the variety of prayer forms together, for example, Patricia Brown, *Paths to Prayer*; Jane Vennard, *A Praying Congregation* or *The Way of Prayer*; Marjorie Thompson, *Soul Feast*; Gary Thomas, *Sacred Pathways*; John Killinger, *Beginning Prayer*. To explore art and spirituality, consider Karla Kincannon, *Creativity and Divine Surprise*; or Christine Valters Paintner and Betsey Beckman, *Awakening the Creative Spirit*.
6. If you can, meet in a place of natural beauty and practice a nature walk as described by Nancy Rowe. How might this form of prayer be shared within your congregation? Consider how time spent in the natural world helps people connect with God. Ask people in your congregation, particularly men, about their experiences in wilderness settings.

CHAPTER 6: INVITING THE SPIRIT INTO SPIRITUAL LIFE MINISTRIES

1. Does one or more of these stories fit in your context? How might it provide a model for you to discern the next steps for a spiritual formation focus in your congregation?

2. Does spiritual formation have a "location" within the organization of your congregation? Does spiritual formation have a "space" within the church building?

3. Return to your definition of *spirituality*. How would your congregation define the term *passionate spirituality*? Name five areas that you would include in the spiritual formation area. Some of these may already be occurring in your small-group or education ministry but have not been named as resourcing spiritual formation.

4. What retreats, events, or conferences might you provide for your congregation and community?

5. How would you address the themes raised in the structure of St. Luke's Spiritual Life Center—(1) development of the inner soul; (2) external connections; (3) infrastructure or administrative issues. Use these three dimensions to help you think about developing your spiritual life ministry into the future.

6. Be realistic. Brainstorm ideas, but then ask, *What is the next step?* Build your program gradually so that you can adjust as you go along.

CHAPTER 7: A NOT-SO-QUIET PENTECOST

1. If possible, plan a half-day or a full-day retreat for your spiritual life team. The location could be a comfortable meeting space in your church, in a team member's home, or at a nearby retreat center.

2. In preparation for reflection, review your notes. Compile any group notes you have into one document to be circulated among the team members. Ask each team member to review these along with their individual notes from the book.

3. Focus on this question: how do we define *spirituality* in our context? Some of the examples in this book have provided a large

umbrella linking spiritual formation, health and wellness, and care ministries. Some have focused on offering small-group experiences, such as studies with Companions in Christ resources. Your answer is what is important for your church and your community.

4. Next, ask this question: are our prayer and spiritual formation ministries primarily for members of our congregation or are they for others in our community? Note that prayer ministries reported here can become outreach opportunities. If you were to reach out, how would you start? If you believe you have more work to do internally with your congregation, what is the next step?

5. Prayerfully play with the concept "spiritual formation as evangelism." How might your spiritual formation opportunities reveal the nature of Christian life to your congregation and community in new ways?

6. Discuss the idea that Jesus desires to guide your congregation in very direct ways. What scriptures would your group suggest as primary to taking this focus seriously?

7. Summarize the group's reflections and name your next steps.

Your team has been engaging in a comprehensive review of the ministries and mission of your congregation and its relationship to your community. Discuss all of your findings with the chairperson of your administrative body and your pastor. Think together about how your discoveries will be shared with your congregation. Prayerfully ask what the continuing role of this task force will be. Perhaps it is time to disband, or perhaps the task force becomes a sustaining visioning group for the congregation.

Celebrate what you have learned together and reflect on how you have been led by the Holy Spirit in this work. Note the key ways you have each been changed personally, as well as the invitations the Holy Spirit has offered to your congregation through this time you have worked together.

Share a meal of blessing together as you envision the next steps you will undertake in the name of Jesus Christ.

NOTES AND SOURCES

INTRODUCTION

1. "What Is Spiritual Formation?" in *The Meeting God Bible* (Nashville, TN: Upper Room Books, 1999), xii.
2. *Lectio divina* means "holy reading" or reading of the divine Word. It is a term used for reading scripture prayerfully and reflectively, with an attitude of seeking meaning directly from the text for personal life. A variety of methods are available for individual and small-group use.
3. Parker J. Palmer, *A Hidden Wholeness: The Journey Toward an Undivided Life* (San Francisco: Jossey-Bass, 2004), 59.
4. John Wesley, "The Means of Grace" (sermon 16), http://gbgm-umc.org/umhistory/wesley/sermons/ (accessed 11/6/12).
5. Thomas Merton, *Contemplative Prayer* (New York: Image Books/Doubleday, 1996), 34–35.

Additional Sources

John Wesley, *A Plain Account of Christian Perfection* (New York: Classic Books America, 2009).

"Nature, Design, and General Rules of the United Societies," *The Book of Discipline of the United Methodist Church 2008* (Nashville, TN: United Methodist Publishing House, 2008), 48–49.

Rueben P. Job, *Three Simple Rules: A Wesleyan Way of Living* (Nashville, TN: Abingdon Press, 2007).

CHAPTER 1

1. Dietrich Bonhoeffer, *The Way to Freedom: Letters, Lectures and Notes, 1935–1939*, from the *Collected Works of Dietrich Bonhoeffer*, vol. 2., ed. Edwin H. Robertson, trans. Edwin H. Robertson and John Bowden (New York: Harper and Row 1966), 57.

2. Morton T. Kelsey, *The Other Side of Silence: Meditation for the Twenty-First Century* (Mahwah, NJ: Paulist Press, 1997); and John A. Sanford, *The Kingdom Within: The Inner Meaning of Jesus' Sayings*, rev. ed. (San Francisco: HarperSanFrancisco, 1987).

3. Walter Wink, *Engaging the Powers: Discernment and Resistance in a World of Domination* (Minneapolis: Augsburg Fortress, 1992).

4. The prayer practices are described in Dwight H. Judy, *Christian Meditation and Inner Healing* (White Sulphur Springs, WV: Order of Saint Luke Publications, 2010). Additional resources studied include Dwight H. Judy, *Embracing God: Praying with Teresa of Avila* (Nashville, TN: Abingdon Press, 1996); and Dwight H. Judy, *Quest for the Mystical Christ: Awakening the Heart of Faith* (Akron, OH: Order of Saint Luke Publications, 2003).

5. Morton T. Kelsey, *Companions on the Inner Way: The Art of Spiritual Guidance* (New York: Crossroad, 1983), 7.

6. *The Collected Works of Saint Teresa of Avila*, trans. Kieran Kavanaugh and Otilio Rodriguez, vol. 2, *The Way of Perfection, Meditations on the Song of Songs, The Interior Castle* (Washington, DC: Institute of Carmelite Studies, 1980), 286.

7. *Alive Now*, Spiritual Tools e-mail for November 2011.

Additional Sources

Norvene Vest, *Gathered in the Word: Praying the Scripture in Small Groups* (Nashville, TN: Upper Room Books), 1996.

http://www.guideposts.org/daily-devotionals (accessed 3/9/12).

Sacred Journey: The Journal of Fellowship in Prayer, *www.fellowshipinprayer.org* (accessed 3/9/12).

David Lowes Watson, *Covenant Discipleship: Christian Formation through Mutual Accountability* (Eugene, OR: Wipf & Stock, 2002).

Steven W. Manskar, *Accountable Discipleship: Living in God's Household* (Nashville, TN: Discipleship Resources, 2003).

Richard Byrd Wilke and Julia Kitchens Wilke, *Disciple: Becoming Disciples Through Bible Study*, Study Manual, 2nd ed. (Nashville, TN: Abingdon Press, 2003).

Corrine Ware, *Discover Your Spiritual Type: A Guide to Individual and Congregational Growth* (Herndon, VA: Alban Institute, 1995).

Linda Douty, *How Can I See the Light When It's So Dark?: Journey to a Thankful Heart* (Harrisburg, PA: Morehouse Publishing, 2007).

Patricia D. Brown, *Paths to Prayer: Finding Your Own Way to the Presence of God* (San Francisco: Jossey-Bass, 2003).

Evelyn Underhill, *Mysticism: The Nature and Development of Spiritual Consciousness* (Chino Valley, AZ: Oneworld, 1999).

Joel Warne, *How to Eat Your Bible: God's Word as Food for Your Soul*, Participant's Guide (Plymouth, MN: WellSpring Life Resources, 2005).

William Johnston, ed., *The Cloud of Unknowing and the Book of Privy Counseling* (Garden City, NY: Image Books/Doubleday, 1973).

Richard J. Foster, *Celebration of Discipline: The Path to Spiritual Growth*, 3rd ed. (San Francisco: HarperSanFrancisco, 1998).

Richard J. Foster and Gayle D. Beebe, *Longing for God: Seven Paths of Christian Devotion* (Downers Grove, IL: InterVarsity Press, 2009).

J. Phillip Newell, *Listening for the Heartbeat of God: A Celtic Spirituality* (Mahwah, NJ: Paulist Press, 1997).

Gerrit Scott Dawson, Adele Gonzalez, E. Glenn Hinson, Rueben P. Job, Marjorie J. Thompson, Wendy M. Wright, *Companions in Christ: A Small-Group Experience in Spiritual Formation* (Nashville, TN: Upper Room Books, 2001).The series was originally published as a 28-week program. In recent years topics have been organized into 8 to 12 week studies.

CHAPTER 2

1. Barbara A. Holmes, *Joy Unspeakable: Contemplative Practices of the Black Church* (Minneapolis: Fortress Press, 2004), 1.

2. Don E. Saliers, *Worship and Spirituality*, Spirituality and the Christian Life (Philadelphia, PA: Westminster Press, 1984), 37–38.

3. Catherine H. Krier, *Symbols for All Seasons: Environmental Planning for Cycles A, B and C* (San Jose, CA: Schuyler Institute for Worship and the Arts, 1988), 28.

4. DeeAnn Klapp, "Biblical Foundations for a Practical Theology of Aging," *Journal of Religious Gerontology* 15, nos. 1/2 (2003): 70.

5. Donna Y. Erickson, "Search for the Memory of God, Pastoral Care with the Cognitively Disabled," chapter 2, Case Study No. 1, in

Wholistic Health Care in the Nursing Home Setting: The Chaplain and the Interdisciplinary Team (D. Min. diss., Luther Seminary), 1999, citing a taped interview between Dr. Melvin Kimble and Viktor Frankl.

6. Marjorie J. Thompson, *Soul Feast: An Invitation to the Christian Spiritual Life* (Louisville, KY: Westminster John Knox Press, 2005), 65–66.

Additional Sources

Paul Konkler, *Don't You Belong to Me?: A Basic Introduction to the Spiritual Life* (New York: Paulist Press, 1979).

The Book of Common Prayer (New York, NY: Church Hymnal Corporation, 1979).

Elise S. Eslinger, compiler and editor, *Upper Room Worshipbook* (Nashville: Upper Room Books, 2002), 233.

Janet L. Aldrich, *Worship for All of God's Children—Worship Liturgy Following the Seasons of the Liturgical Year Designed for Memory-impaired Older Adults,* D.Min. project, Garrett-Evangelical Theological Seminary, Evanston, Illinois, May 2008.

Valerie E. Hess and Marti Watson Garlett, *Habits of a Child's Heart: Raising Your Kids with the Spiritual Disciplines* (Colorado Springs, CO: NavPress, 2004).

Adele Ahlberg Calhoun, *Spiritual Disciplines Handbook: Practices That Transform Us* (Downers Grove, IL: InterVarsity Press, 2005).

CHAPTER 3

1. See Jane Tomaine, *St. Benedict's Toolbox: The Nuts and Bolts of Everyday Benedictine Living* (Harrisburg, PA: Morehouse Publishing, 2005).

2. Gary D. Kinnaman and Alfred H. Ells, *Leaders That Last: How Covenant Friendships Can Help Pastors Thrive* (Grand Rapids, MI: Baker Books, 2003), 64.

3. W. Paul Jones, *The Art of Spiritual Direction: Giving and Receiving Spiritual Guidance* (Nashville, TN: Upper Room Books, 2002), 223.

4. Charles M. Olsen, *Transforming Church Boards into Communities of Spiritual Leaders* (Bethesda, MD: Alban Institute, 1995), xiii.

5. Ibid., 26.

6. Ibid., 7.

7. Ibid., 14.

8. See Robert Schnase, *Five Practices of Fruitful Congregations* (Nashville, TN: Abingdon Press, 2007). Schnase names the five practices as radical hospitality, passionate worship, intentional faith development, risk-taking mission and service, and extravagant generosity.

9. Mary Poplin, *Finding Calcutta: What Mother Teresa Taught Me About Meaningful Work and Service* (Downers Grove, IL: InterVarsity Press, 2008), 13.

10. For use as individual discernment, the process is described in Dwight H. Judy, *Discerning Life Transitions: Listening Together in Spiritual Direction* (New York: Morehouse Publishing, 2010).

Additional Sources

Benedict of Nursia, *The Rule of St. Benedict* trans. Anthony C. Meisel and M. L. del Mastro (New York: Image Doubleday, 1975).

Martin Luther King Jr., *Letter from the Birmingham Jail* (New York: HarperCollins, 1994).

CHAPTER 4

1. *www.StudentOpenCircles.com* (accessed 2/20/12).

2. *www.24-7prayer.org* (accessed 1/23/2012).

3. Andy Freeman and Pete Greig, *Punk Monk: New Monasticism and the Ancient Art of Breathing* (Ventura, CA: Regal Books, 2007), 14.

4. Richard J. Foster, *Streams of Living Water: Celebrating the Great Traditions of Christian Faith* (San Francisco: HarperSanFrancisco, 1998), 25.

5. See Nicola Slee, *Women's Faith Development: Patterns and Processes* (Burlington, VT: Ashgate Publishing, 2004); Evelyn L. Parker, *The Sacred Selves of Adolescent Girls: Hard Stories of Race, Class, and Gender* (Eugene, OR: Wipf & Stock, 2010); Joyce Ann Mercer, *Girl Talk/God Talk: Why Faith Matters to Teenage Girls—and Their Parents* (San Francisco: Jossey-Bass, 2008).

6. Christine Valters Paintner and Betsey Beckman, *Awakening the Creative Spirit: Bringing the Arts to Spiritual Direction* (Harrisburg, PA: Morehouse Publishing, 2010), 3.

7. Ibid., 214.

8. Eden Alternative website, *http://www.edenalt.org/about-the-eden-alternative* (accessed 3/15/12).

9. Judy, *Discerning Life Transitions*, 69.

10. Eugene C. Bianchi, *Aging as a Spiritual Journey* (New York: Crossroad Publishing, 1982), 178.

11. Gene D. Cohen, *The Creative Age: Awaking Human Potential in the Second Half of Life* (New York: Avon Books, 2000), 7, 10.

12. Randy Maddox, *Responsible Grace: John Wesley's Practical Theology* (Nashville, TN: Kingswood Books/Abingdon Press, 1994), 153.

13. Bianchi, *Aging as a Spiritual Journey*, 207.

14. "Blessed Assurance," *The United Methodist Hymnal* (Nashville, TN: The United Methodist Publishing House, 1989), no. 369.

15. Brian D. McLaren, *Naked Spirituality: A Life with God in 12 Simple Words* (New York: HarperOne, 2011), 223.

16. *http://www.fumcomaha.org/#/mercy-justice/health-ministries* (accessed 11/24/12).

Additional Sources

Pete Greig and Dave Roberts, *Red Moon Rising: How 24-7 Prayer Is Awakening a Generation* (Lake Mary, FL: Relevant Books, 2003).

CHAPTER 5

1. Jane E. Vennard, *A Praying Congregation: The Art of Teaching Spiritual Practice* (Herndon, VA: Alban Institute, 2005), 113.

2. Brown, *Paths to Prayer*, v–vii.

3. Rev. Tom Albin is dean of Upper Room Ministries and Ecumenical Relations, Nashville, Tennessee.

4. *http://www.contemplativeoutreach.org/* see website for resources noted (accessed 3/1/12).

5. Thomas Keating, *Open Mind, Open Heart*, 20th-anniversary ed. (New York: Continuum International, 2006); J. David Muyskens, *Forty Days to a Closer Walk with God: The Practice of Centering Prayer* (Nashville, TN: Upper Room Books, 2006); Cynthia Bourgeault, *Centering Prayer and Inner Awakening* (Cambridge, MA: Cowley Publications, 2004).

6. Additional resources on the labyrinth: Labyrinth Society, *http://labyrinthsociety.org;* and Veriditas™, *http://veriditas.org/* (accessed 11/6/12).

7. For fuller description, see Nancy Mangano Rowe, "Walking on Sacred Soil: In Memory of Thomas Berry," *Presence: An International Journal of Spiritual Direction* 17, no. 2 (June 2011).

8. For a description, see chapter 4, "Meditating on God in Creation," in Dwight H. Judy, *Christian Meditation and Inner Healing* (White Sulphur Springs, WV: OSL Publications, 2010).

9. Anthony Mottola, trans., *The Spiritual Exercises of Saint Ignatius* (New York: Image Books/Doubleday, 1989), 72.

Additional Sources

Ron DelBene, Mary Montgomery, and Herb Montgomery, *The Hunger of the Heart: A Call to Spiritual Growth—A Daily Workbook for Use in Groups* (Eugene, OR: Wipf & Stock, 2005).

Richard Rohr and Andreas Ebert, *The Enneagram: A Christian Perspective* (New York: Crossroad Publishing, 2001).

Don Richard Riso and Russ Hudson, *Discovering Your Personality Type: The Essential Introduction to the Enneagram*, rev. ed. (Boston: Houghton Mifflin, 2003).

William Johnston, ed., *The Cloud of Unknowing and Book of Privy Counseling.*

Lauren Artress, *Walking a Sacred Path: Rediscovering the Labyrinth as a Spiritual Practice*, rev. ed. (New York: Riverhead Books, 2006).

Thomas Berry, *The Sacred Universe: Earth, Spirituality, and Religion in the Twenty-first Century*, ed. Mary Evelyn Tucker (New York: Columbia University Press, 2009).

Thich Nhat Hanh, *Peace Is Every Step: The Path of Mindfulness in Everyday Life*, ed. Arnold Kotler (New York: Bantam Books, 1992).

Karla M. Kincannon, *Creativity and Divine Surprise: Finding the Place of Your Resurrection* (Nashville, TN: Upper Room Books, 2005).

Paintner and Beckman, *Awakening the Creative Spirit.*

N. Graham Standish, *Forming Faith in a Hurricane: A Spiritual Primer for Daily Living* (Nashville, TN: Upper Room Books, 1998).

Robert Moore and Douglas Gillette, *King, Warrior, Magician, Lover: Rediscovering the Archetypes of the Mature Masculine* (New York: HarperCollins, 1991).

Richard Rohr, *Adam's Return: The Five Promises of Male Initiation* (New York: Crossroad Publishing, 2004).

http://4gatewayscoaching.com/ (accesssed 3/1/12).

Gary Thomas, *Sacred Pathways: Discover Your Soul's Path to God*, updated and expanded (Grand Rapids, MI: Zondervan, 1996, 2010).

CHAPTER 6

1. *The Book of Discipline of The United Methodist Church* (Nashville, TN: United Methodist Publishing House, 2008), 72.

2. *www.lifehouseministriesinc.com* (accessed 3/2/12).

3. *www.stlukesumc.com* (accessed 3/2/12).

4. Robert Benson, *Daily Prayer: A Simple Plan for Learning to Say the Daily Prayer of the Church* DVD & CD (Raleigh, NC: Carolina Broadcasting, 2006); John F. DeVries, *Why Pray?: 40 Days—from Words to Relationship* (Tulsa, OK: Honor Books, 2005); Foster, *Streams of Living Water*; Henri J.M. Nouwen, *Making All Things New: An Invitation to the Spiritual Life* (San Francisco: HarperSanFrancisco, 1981); Henri J.M. Nouwen, *With Open Hands*, 2nd ed. (Notre Dame, IN: Ave Maria Press, 2006); James Bryan Smith and Lynda Graybeal, *A Spiritual Formation Workbook: Small-Group Resources for Nurturing Christian Growth*, rev. ed. (San Francisco: HarperSanFrancisco, 1999).

5. Diana Butler Bass, *Christianity for the Rest of Us: How the Neighborhood Church Is Transforming the Faith* (New York: HarperOne, 2006), 6.

6. Diana Butler Bass, *Christianity after Religion: The End of Church and the Birth of a New Spiritual Awakening* (New York: HarperOne, 2012).

Additional Sources

Christian Schwarz, *Natural Church Development: A Guide to Eight Essential Qualities of Healthy Churches* (St. Charles, IL: Churchsmart Resources, 1996).

Schnase, *Five Practices of Fruitful Congregations*.

Dawson and others, *Companions in Christ.*

Marjorie J. Thompson, *Exploring the Way: An Introduction to the Spiritual Journey*, Participant's Book (Nashville, TN: Upper Room Books, 2005).

Marjorie J. Thompson and Stephen D. Bryant, *The Way of Blessedness* (Nashville, TN: Upper Room Books, 2003).

Doughty and Thompson, *The Way of Discernment.*

Thompson, *Soul Feast.*

M. Robert Mulholland Jr., *Invitation to a Journey: A Road Map for Spiritual Formation* (Downers Grove, IL: InterVarsity Press, 1993).

Judy, *Discerning Life Transitions.*

Foster, *Celebration of Discipline.*

Jane E. Vennard, *Be Still: Designing and Leading Contemplative Retreats* (Herndon, VA: Alban Institute, 2000).

CHAPTER 7

1. Schnase, *Five Practices of Fruitful Congregations*, 31.

2. *http://cjmission.org/* (accessed 3/1/12).

3. Hearts on Fire: Fellowship of United Methodist Spiritual Directors and Retreat Leaders. *http://fumsdrl.org/* (accessed 3/12/12); Spiritual Directors International. *http://www.sdiworld.org/* (accessed 3/12/12).

4. Elizabeth O'Connor, *Call to Commitment: The Story of the Church of the Saviour, Washington, DC* (New York: Harper & Row, 1963), 85.

5. Thomas Merton, *Contemplative Prayer*, 34–35.

Additional Sources

Smith and Graybeal, *A Spiritual Formation Workbook.*

DeVries, *Why Pray?*

Ernest Boyer Jr., *A Way in the World: Family Life as Spiritual Discipline* (New York: HarperCollins, 1984).

Brown, *Paths to Prayer.*

Chester P. Michael and Marie C. Norrisey, *Prayer and Temperament: Different Prayer Forms for Different Personality Types* (Charlottesville, VA: Open Door, 1984).

Foster, *Streams of Living Water.*

Thompson, *Soul Feast.*

Palmer, *A Hidden Wholeness.*

Danny E. Morris and Charles M. Olsen, *Discerning God's Will Together: A Spiritual Practice for the Church* (Nashville, TN: Upper Room Books, 1999).

Gordon T. Smith, *The Voice of Jesus: Discernment, Prayer and the Witness of the Spirit* (Downers Grove, IL: InterVarsity Press, 2003).

CONTRIBUTORS

CHAPTER 1

Janna Born Larsen, Pastoral Ministries Manager and Chaplain, Sedgebrook Community, a Continuing Care Retirement Community, Lincolnshire, Illinois

Rev. Marianne Chalstrom, Elder (retired), Indiana Conference, United Methodist Church

Rev. Dr. Randall R. Hansen, Montague United Methodist Church, Montague, Michigan

Rev. Beth Fender, New Streams, Illinois Great Rivers Conference, United Methodist Church

Rev. Dr. Rebecca Laird, Associate Professor of Christian Ministry and Practice, School of Theology and Christian Ministry, Point Loma Nazarene University, San Diego, California

Rev. J. Richard Wilson, University Park United Methodist Church, Dallas, Texas

Joanne B. Knight, Christ Church Cathedral (Episcopal), Nashville, Tennessee

Nancy LeValley, Coordinator of Spiritual Formation, Traverse Bay United Methodist Church, Traverse City, Michigan

Rev. Jeff Cover, Associate Pastor, Central Presbyterian Church, Lafayette, Indiana

CHAPTER 2

Rev. Dr. Leroy Cothran, United Missionary Baptist Church, Dayton, Ohio

Suzanne Clement, Franklin, Tennessee

Rev. Dr. Janet L. Aldrich, Chaplain, Presbyterian Homes, Evanston, Illinois

Nancy E. Dibelius

Stacey Gassman, M.Div.

Rev. Dean Francis, Senior Pastor, First United Methodist Church, Evanston, Illinois

Lowell G. Black, Pastor of Spiritual Formation, First United
Methodist Church, Valparaiso, Indiana
Rev. Sheryl Palmer, Saint John's United Methodist Church,
Edwardsville, Illinois
James Denton, Certified Elder Candidate, Indiana Conference, the
United Methodist Church

CHAPTER 3

Rev. Dr. Brenda Buckwell, First United Methodist Church,
Zanesville, Ohio
Rev. Brian K. White, Southeast District, Indiana Conference, United
Methodist Church
Rev. Eugenia A. Gamble, Nipomo Community Presbyterian Church
Pastor Gene Turner and Sharon Hicks, Stronghurst and Carman
United Methodist Churches, Stronghurst and Carman, Illinois
Cindy Serio, Deacon, United Methodist Church

CHAPTER 4

Marybeth Leis and Jeff Druery, Student Open Circles, McMaster
University, Hamilton, Ontario, Canada
Rev. Jennie Edwards Bertrand, United Methodist Campus Ministry,
Illinois State University
Melanie S. Baffes
Steve Braudt, Associate Pastor for Youth and College, First United
Methodist Church, Cedar Falls, Iowa
Janna Born Larsen, Pastoral Ministries Manager and Chaplain,
Sedgebrook Community, a Continuing Care Retirement
Community, Lincolnshire, Illinois
Susan D. Amick, Chaplain, Sanctuary at Bellbrook, Rochester Hills,
Michigan
Kay McLellan, R.N., B.S.N., Faith United Presbyterian Church,
Farmers Branch, Texas

CHAPTER 5

Rev. Eugenia A. Gamble, Nipomo Community Presbyterian Church

Helen Stegall, Deacon, Arkansas Conference, United Methodist Church

Mary L. Hooper, Central United Methodist Church, Meridian, Mississippi

Marjorie Donnelly, M.Ed., Director of Christian Formation, Holy Trinity Episcopal Church, Greensboro, North Carolina

Rev. Glynden Bode, Spirit's Call Ministries, Houston, Texas

Rev. Nancy Mangano Rowe, Ph.D., Sofia University (formerly Institute of Transpersonal Psychology)

Rev. Karla M. Kincannon, Director of Field Education and Vocational Formation and Church Leadership, Garrett-Evangelical Theological Seminary, Evanston, Illinois

Rev. J. Todd Smiedendorf, Washington Park United Church of Christ, Denver, Colorado

CHAPTER 6

Cherri Johnson, First United Methodist Church, Baton Rouge, Louisiana

Rev. Cathy Brewton, LifeHouse Ministries, Ruston, Louisiana

Betty Brandt, Saint Luke's United Methodist Church, Indianapolis, Indiana

Rev. Rosie Helms, Deacon (retired), Indiana Conference, United Methodist Church

Jane Watts, Jackson, Mississippi

Diane Stephens, Spiritual Director and a Ruling Elder in the Presbyterian Church (U.S.A.)

Shelagh Donoghue, Saint Francis Xavier, Wilmette, Illinois

CHAPTER 7

Rev. Rosie Helms, Deacon (retired), Indiana Conference, United Methodist Church

Rev. Sheila Wilson-Freelon, Esq., M.Div., Pastor, Turner Memorial
AME Church and Director of Evangelism, South District Chicago
Conference, Fourth Episcopal District African Methodist
Episcopal Church, Chicago, Illinois

Jane Watts

Barbara A. Hale

Rev. Janis Blean-Kachigan, Formation Tending, Milwaukee,
Wisconsin

Rev. John E. Anderson, D.Min., Trinity Presbyterian Church,
Arvada, Colorado

ABOUT THE AUTHOR

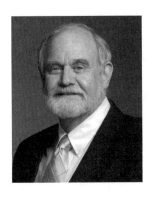

Dwight H. Judy is Professor Emeritus of Spiritual Formation and founding director of the Rueben Job Institute for Spiritual Formation at Garrett-Evangelical Seminary in Evanston, Illinois. He has served as a parish pastor in the North Texas Conference of the United Methodist Church, a retreat leader, faculty member for the Institute of Transpersonal Psychology and for the Academy for Spiritual Formation (The Upper Room). He is a member of Spiritual Directors International and the American Association of Pastoral Counselors. He offers retreats nationally and sees individuals in spiritual direction.

Dr. Judy received his BA degree from Southern Methodist University, his MTh from Perkins School of Theology, and his PhD from the Institute of Transpersonal Psychology.

Previous books include *Discerning Life Transitions: Listening Together in Spiritual Direction*; *Christian Meditation and Inner Healing*; *Embracing God: Praying with Teresa of Avila*; *Quest for the Mystical Christ: Awakening the Heart of Faith*; and *Healing the Male Soul: Christianity and the Mythic Journey*.

Dwight and his wife, Ruth, are parents of two grown sons.

Visit Dwight Judy at http://www.dwightjudy.com

MORE TITLES FROM UPPER ROOM BOOKS

Companions in Christ
A Small-Group Experience in Spiritual Formation
initial series
- *Embracing the Journey: The Way of Christ* 978-0-8358-9830-0
- *Feeding on the Word: The Mind of Christ* 978-0-8358-9831-7
- *Deepening Our Prayer: The Heart of Christ* 978-0-8358-9832-4
- *Responding to Our Call: The Work of Christ* 978-0-8358-9833-1
- *Exploring Spiritual Guidance: The Spirit of Christ* 978-0-8358-9834-8
- *Leader's Guide* 978-0-8358-9840-9

Beginning Prayer, John Killinger • 978-0-8358-1186-6

*Creativity and Divine Surprise: Finding the Place of Your Resur-
rection*, Karla M. Kincannon • 978-0-8358-9812-6

The Cycle of Grace: Living in Sacred Balance, Trevor Hudson and
Jerry P. Haas • 978-0-8358-1198-9

*Forty Days to a Closer Walk with God: The Practice of Centering
Prayer*, J. David Muyskens • 978-0-8358-9904-8

"Pray for Me": The Power in Praying for Others,
Kenneth H. Carter Jr. • 978-0-8358-1090-6

A Spirituality of Fundraising, Henri J.M. Nouwen •
978-0-8358-1044-9

A Spirituality of Living, Henri J.M. Nouwen •
978-0-8358-1088-3

Time Away: A Guide for Personal Retreat, Ben Campbell
Johnson and Paul H. Lang • 978-0-8358-1011-1

The Upper Room *Disciplines*, annual publication of daily
devotions based on the Lectionary readings, multiple authors

To learn more about these and other Upper Room
resources, visit our website and bookstore
books.upperroom.org/ • bookstore.upperroom.org/
or call 1.800.972.0433